THE BATTLE ❄

❄ on

SNOWSHOES ❄

Bob Bearor

Joe Lee
96

HERITAGE BOOKS, INC.

Published 1997 by

HERITAGE BOOKS, INC.
1540E Pointer Ridge Place
Bowie, Maryland 20716
1-800-398-7709

ISBN 0-7884-0619-1

A Complete Catalog Listing Hundreds of Titles
On History, Genealogy, and Americana
Available Free Upon Request

This book is dedicated to my father

BERT BEAROR

It was Dad who instilled in me the love of history, the love of the woods, and the pride of our ancestors.

CONTENTS_____

LIST OF MAPS AND PHOTOGRAPHS ⸻

ACKNOWLEDGMENTS

THE saying, "No man is an island," is particularly appropriate when undertaking the writing of a book. No author ever successfully created a book without the help of many others. I would like to take this opportunity to thank those special people who made this book possible.

First to my wife, Holly, and my daughters, Jenny and Becky, for their patience, encouragement, and support throughout these past years of researching and writing.

To my sons, Cliff and Ted, who have shared many events, camps, hunts, and trips throughout the years. Two finer companions I could not ask for. I hope the years ahead are as much fun as the years gone by.

Much of the credit for making this book a reality is due to the efforts of my proofreader, Dorothy Jacobson, and my typist, Carol Schrom. These two fine women were able to take my scribblings, scratchings, notes, documents, and thoughts and put them together into a piece of work that I am proud of. The bulk of the labor fell upon these two ladies, and they willingly and cheerfully helped make this book possible.

Thanks to Monique Champagne Serafin who translated all the French letters, documents, and correspondence for me.

I am especially grateful to Nick Westbrook, Director of Fort Ticonderoga; Bruce Mosely, Curator; and Delight Gartlein and all the staff at the fort and its research center. Their help, suggestions, encouragement, and friendliness made a difficult job a joy to accomplish.

I am indebted to the late Roger De Chame for the sharing of his time and immense knowledge of the Ticonderoga area. Roger and I covered many miles in our trips to the battle site, patrol trails, and historic locations. Roger also showed to me the site of the French advanced post of Coutre Coeur, the exact spot where Langy was wounded crossing the Ticonderoga River after the death of Lord Howe; and the location of the site of the 1757 French ambush of Rogers in a minor snowshoe battle that foreshadowed the one yet to come.

Special thanks go to Steve Caporizzo, WTEN meteorologist, who helped me to accurately depict the weather and climate, based on the recordings taken from Albany to Montreal in the years 1757-1758.

My Ranger research was made possible by the three most widely recognized Ranger experts of today: Gary Zaboly, Burt Loescher, and George Alfred Bray III. Thanks, guys, for sharing your knowledge and ideas.

The same thanks go to George "Pesckunck" Larrabee for his help in researching and describing the Indians' arms and equipment. George is well known among muzzleloading enthusiasts for his historical magazine articles, and is also an adopted member of the Abenaki Indian Nation of northern Vermont. George was instrumental in bringing the authentic Native Americans to our photo session this winter.

My French research was helped immeasurably by the knowledge of Andre Gousse and Steve DeLisle of the Milice de Chambly; Andrew Gallup and Donald "Doc" Shaffer, co-authors of *La Marine: The French Colonial Soldier in Canada, 1745-1761*; and Barbara and Philip Howard of Le Troupes de La Pointe de Chevelure.

Thanks to the members of the Ethan Allen Long Rifle Club of Vermont, who helped organize and schedule the picture event, especially Wight Manning, Mike and Debera Blakeslee, and Rich and Karen Rathbun.

From myself and all the members of the E.A.L.R.C., a deep and personal "Thank You" goes to the Roger Layn family of Monkton, Vermont, for the use of their lands for our shoots, war games, and re-enactment events. Their sharing of nature's beautiful resources is a treasure indeed.

Thanks to brother firefighter and New York State Outdoor Guides Association member Ed Murphy for helping me in the planning of my winter trek, and for pointing out the dangers of Lake George ice travel.

Thanks go to Greg Geiger, who has been my muzzleloading companion for many years, and who has helped me with ideas for this book from his own experience as a published author.

Thanks also to John Gunning, Floyd Densmore, Dean Cook, the Ticonderoga Country Club, and many other residents of the town of Ticonderoga, who allowed me the permission to do my extensive field research trips.

I am deeply indebted to my photographer, Al Cederstrom, for his skill, ingenuity, and expertise in creating the authentic battle scenes in the book. Without Al's pictures, this book would not have "come to life" for the readers to enjoy.

Finally, to all of the re-enactors listed below, who traveled from all over the northeastern United States and Canada to answer the call for the photo session, I extend my deepest thanks.

ENGLISH FORCES - Jim Ross, Horst Dressler, Mike Barbieri, Richard Callahan, Jeremy Nemeth, Jim Bezio, Greg Butler, Thomas Wolenc, David Fenn, Steve Halford, Alan Bassett, and Albert Smith.

NATIVE AMERICANS - George "Pesckunck" Larrabee, Ray "Running Bear" Brow, Charlie "Two Feathers" Correll, Ben Goodrich, Charles "Mountain Bear" Schongar Sr., Charles W. Schongar Jr., and Daryl Curran.

FRENCH FORCES - Cliff Bearor, Ted Bearor, Thomas Howard, Phillip Howard, Wight Manning, Mike Blakeslee, Paul Blakeslee, Russ Spies, Bill Wade, Dave Wren, Greg Geiger, Andre Gousse, and Emmanuel Nivon.

Finally, since she had the last word on everything, and used it well, I express my deepest gratitude to Roxanne Carlson, senior editor of Heritage Books, Inc. Roxanne has taken a good book, and made it much better. Thanks, Roxanne.

FOREWORD

December 1995

By Nicholas Westbrook
Director, Fort Ticonderoga

ROBERT ROGERS of the Rangers endures as one of the "larger-than-life" characters of our colonial history. In the hearts of his comrades in arms, he mustered that respect through heroic action and charismatic leadership. In the imaginations of his contemporaries, he achieved that stature through the skillful creation of his own exotic celebrity as frontiersman, warrior, even playwright, beginning with his *Reminiscences*. Since then, two centuries of biography, folk tales, and geographical place names have amplified his mythic nature.

Here in Ticonderoga, Robert Rogers has been with us for 240 years, always challenging and inspiring, usually exasperating and annoying—sometimes in victory, sometimes in defeat. Perhaps his most vividly recalled action near Ticonderoga was the "Battle on Snowshoes" in March 1758; a disastrous prelude to the equally disastrous summer campaign led by Major General Abercromby.

Re-enactor and historian Bob Bearor retells that story, but with a significant difference. For most of the past 240 years, the story of that battle has focused on Rogers. Strangely, somehow in the telling his disaster manages to sound almost like a victory. The enemy is usually an anonymous collection of "French and Indians," with little more nuance or individuality. But here you will find the spotlight dramatically shifted to Rogers' opponent, Langis—that is, Ensign Jean-Baptiste Levrault de Langis de Montegron of the Compagnie Franche de la Marine. Langis, a gifted Canadian partisan leader, was never bested in all his confrontations with Rogers and the Rangers. The Battle on Snowshoes was no exception. Bob Bearor shows us how and why.

The story comes alive through his personal style, careful research, and insight drawn from personal experience as a re-enactor in these hills and valleys. Bob Bearor's lively account draws our attention to Langis and *his* partisans. Here is the Battle on Snowshoes as you have not seen it before.

PREFACE

IN all probability the idea for this book was born more than forty years ago, in August 1954, when my dad took me to Fort Ticonderoga for the first time. He bought me a toy flintlock musket and told me about the history of the fort, the French and Indian War, and the Battle on Snowshoes.

Since the 1960's I have purchased or borrowed every book I could find that dealt with the Battle of Snowshoes. I am fortunate to have access today to as much and even more information than the great early writers such as Francis Parkman or Burt G. Loescher ever had. People more fluent in French than myself have translated the many letters and documents regarding the battle.

I am fortunate to live only an hour's drive from the battle site. As a result I have been able to spend more time at the various locations than is possible for most people today. Five years of extensive field research was relatively easy for me to be able to accomplish.

Some who read this book may feel that my views are somewhat prejudiced in favor of the French, simply because I am of French Canadian descent. Not so. Any different descriptions and evaluations of the battle are just that. Different. The only versions of this story previously available were strictly those written from the English and American perspectives.

Finally, now that nearly 240 years have passed since the Battle on Snowshoes, it's doubtful that further research would uncover any previously unknown information. But nothing is impossible. If any new or contrasting evidence should ever be found and made known, I would be among the first to wish to receive it.

INTRODUCTION

WHILE writing this book I chose to use phrases such as "probably," "perhaps," "may have," and "entirely possible" for good reasons. I also tried to avoid the use of the word "never." Let me explain why.

The clothing, arms, and equipment that I described were available in that period to those particular groups of men. Whether or not they used them, or something else, is a moot point. They "could have" and "probably did." It is easy to write about history that is documented. It is also very dry. For instance, it is well documented that General Edward Braddock had horses shot out from under him in the battle at the Monongahela. What kind of horses (mares or stallions), or what colors (chestnut, gray, or black), is unknown and really unimportant for a writer who is trying to inject a sense of life and background to a story, as I did in the "Battle" chapter. It is more dangerous for a person to proclaim definitely that they did not wear or "never" wore a certain outfit, if in fact the clothing was available in those days.

Some examples of the word "never" that I have encountered in various forms from self-proclaimed re-enactment "experts" of today will serve to make the point. Years ago I was told by an individual who billed his group as the "most authentic French unit in North America" that the French partisan leaders, such as Langy and Joseph Marin, would "never" have worn a tricorne hat in the woods when raiding the frontiers. Let's shoot some holes in that theory. Tricornes, round hats, *tuques*, Canadian fur caps, and *bonnets du police*, were all available to the French troops who went on frontier raids. I believe a man wore a hat that was his personal preference, and/or whatever was available to him at the time.

Fred Gowen, from Massachusetts, does more period trekking (living and traveling in the woods) than anyone else I know. Together we have shared many camps and trails. Fred prefers the round felt hat, while my choice is the tricorne. Both shade the eyes somewhat in the sunlight, both are less apt to get plucked off by every little branch or twig (like the soft wool of a tuque), and both are better suited in the rain, acting like a small umbrella. In real cold weather we both tie silk scarves over our heads and around our ears, putting the hats on top. At night I have a woolen bonnet du police, made from the same material as my *justacorps* coat, that I pull over my head for warmth while sleeping. As an added thought on the French wearing tricornes on frontier raids, I would point out that many paintings of that period contain figures of men wearing tricornes.

Another interesting "never" from this same individual was addressed to my sons and myself (who dress as French partisan leaders) at a recent Fort Niagara encampment. He informed us that French officers would never dress "barechested," or "dress down like the Indians. They always wore shirts and uniforms, in the forts or in the brush." As I pointed out to this individual, he would do well to read the accounts of James Smith, an English boy captured by the Indians and held prisoner at Fort Duquesne prior to Braddock's defeat. From his perch in Fort Duquesne, Smith gave an accurate description and count of the French force that went out to defeat Braddock's army that day in July 1755. He described how the leader of the French force, Captain Daniel de Beaujeu, stripped to the waist, painted himself like the Indians, and, after receiving the blessing and communion from Father Denys, led out his mixed group of French and Indians with only the gorget on his chest that identified him as a white officer. Later on that day the English engineer, Harry Gordon, who was in the British advance corps, was the first of Braddock's men to see the French force coming towards them at a run. (O'Meara, p. 144.) The leader was described as "A white man dressed as an Indian, but wearing a shining gorget." (Hamilton, p. 156.) This incident is well recorded in many books of history which anyone can easily purchase or obtain from libraries, museums, and research centers, just as are the accounts of the Battle on Snowshoes.

The opinions that I share with you, the reader, are based not only on book research but actual field experiences. Just as George Plimpton, author of the book on professional football *Paper Lion*, and Robin Moore, who underwent training for his book, *The Green Berets*, wanted to experience for themselves the subject that they wrote about, I chose to do the same, to give credence to this work. Short of being in a live snowshoe battle (I've done re-enactments), I've trekked over the sites in period clothing and equipment, made countless camps throughout the hills (even one during March when the temperature was minus 20°), searched out travel routes, and tried to substantiate times and recorded journal entries. Because of this, I feel that I can separate fact from fiction as accurately as possible.

For instance, when I tell you that the French force leaving Fort Ticonderoga on snowshoes would take two hours to arrive at Trout Brook, I know that for a fact, because I did it, in eighteenth-century clothing and equipment, on snowshoes, in three feet of snow. While other writers speak of a trail that the French patrolled daily through the mountains, I can show you exactly where it was, where it went, and how long it took, because my son Cliff and I spent days following it.

On Monday, March 13 (the exact anniversary day of the battle), I re-created Rogers' day exactly as stated in his journals. I cached my hand sleigh and blankets at the exact site where he left his under guard. I then proceeded through the woods and swamps and lands where the Rangers had walked (with owners' permission) to the battle site, arriving exactly at 3:30 P.M. I spent the next few hours contemplating the scene and area of the ambush and battle until dusk finally started settling in. At six o'clock, as the surrounding woods turned gloomy, I started back along the highway of Route 9N, which was the most likely route followed by the fleeing Rangers, towards the rendezvous site, four miles distant. It took me about two hours of steady walking to cover the distance. As I walked along, the light of an almost full moon helped immeasurably to put to rest other wives' tales about the pursuit of Rogers by the savages. While walking alongside the road, and in the open fields, my tracks in the snow were somewhat easily visible. (Written accounts in *Rogers' Reminiscences* reveal that there *was* moonlight on the night of the battle.) However, as soon as I cut across the country and entered the forest with its overhanging canopy of pine, hemlock, and spruce limbs, the tracks were VERY difficult to follow, all the while keeping mindful presence to avoid the low hanging branches and twigs that poked at my eyes and face. I also realized that while I was able to slowly follow the tracks, I was not in any danger of having my body tenderized by a load of buckshot from up ahead. My opinion was definitely re-inforced that the Indians would not have been so foolish as to give chase in the dark. I chose to illustrate this point on p. 65, with a true story from my own experience as the basis for the bear chase of Langy's childhood memory. There is no documented case of such an event occurring in Langy's life, though such a thing certainly could have happened.

There is a story that claims Rogers finally escaped by sliding down the stony escarpment known today as Rogers Rock. One of many ways of putting to rest this tale was manifesting itself on this trip back to the site: the time element. If the battle had ended with darkness, around six o'clock (as both sides stated), and Rogers had "arrived on the ice at eight P.M.," he could not possibly have had the time to snowshoe three miles, and then taken the time and effort to struggle and climb up the steep western slopes of Rogers Rock. Again I ask, why would he? His rendezvous was at the southern end of the mountain; the fastest and easiest trails were back over his original route, or using the trail over the slight pass to Hearts Bay and down the lake from there. This tale of folklore is just that, a tale which has entertained and been magnified through the years, to fire people's imaginations and to sell books. There is absolutely no doubt or hesitancy in my mind, that it never happened. It is simply a good tale that got better.

I reached the rendezvous site at about eight P.M. and uncovered the sleigh. I ate some cold rations washed down with brandy and water. As I wrapped up in my blankets under the stars, I thought to myself, "How were these men able to pass the night without contracting hypothermia?" Remember, they had dropped their packs on the slopes, and advanced to the ambush site at the stream. Because of the speed and savagery of the ambush and their ensuing retreat up the hill, it is unlikely that any of them had a chance to recover their packs or coats. Also, at the rendezvous site, they were not allowed to have fires for fear of discovery by the French. So how did they survive? One of two ways: either there were extra blankets on the cached hand sleighs (very possible and probable), or they had to bunch tightly together in a mass, to retain body heat. After three days of physically demanding marching, fighting a battle, seeing the horror of most of their force getting wiped out, and running for their lives in the evening without warm outer clothing, the difficulty of spending the night without fire must have been indescribable.

As I continued my musings that evening, I recalled the elegant prose of Francis Parkman in his book *Montcalm and Wolfe:*

> "Like Dürer's Knight, a ghastly death stalked ever at his side. There were those among them for whom this stern life had a fascination that made all other existence tame."
>
> (Parkman, p. 302.)

And really, that sums up the forest fighters of both sides in this battle. Nobody ordered these men, any of them, to go on this mission. The Rangers, and the accompanying British regulars, were all volunteers. The Canadians, the Indians, and the soldiers of La Reine and La Marine, all asked to go. All the men who fought in the Battle on Snowshoes chose to be there willingly. For the soldiers of the fort it was a chance to do something exciting, to break up the monotony of winter garrison life. For the Canadians it was a chance to carry the fight to the English, a chance for adventure and glory. For the Indians it was simply an opportunity to kill, scalp, and plunder, to do deeds that could be re-told at the council fires in years to come. For the Rangers and British it was much the same motive; a challenge to gain victory and honor, and perhaps the opportunity to take a scalp for the profit of a five-pound sterling note [$25.00]. They all were cut out of the same cloth.

Finally, as fatigue settled in, I drifted off to a fitful night's sleep. I awoke shivering in my blankets the next morning, at the site where Rogers and the remnants of his Rangers had passed the cold terrible night, and as dawn appeared I looked over the snow- and ice-covered lake. Amidst the tomb-like silence, I could easily picture Rogers leading his broken force back down the lake. I can only imagine the suffering that was endured in the very spot where I had spent the previous night. Cold, wounded, exhausted and frightened men; terribly beaten, fearful of French troops coming upon them, yet staying as long as they dared for any of their comrades who might make it back in time.

I rolled up my blankets, took a drink of brandy in salute to those brave men of both sides, and then headed back towards home. The research was over; it was time to write the book.

PROLOGUE ───────────────

THE Battle. It was fought in the late winter of 1758, about halfway through the conflict known as the Seven Years' War, or more commonly known as the French and Indian War.

In the early years of that war the French achieved several great victories, with Braddock's defeat in 1755, and the capture and destruction of Fort Oswego in 1756 and Fort William Henry in 1757. The year 1758 brought the last of the great French victories at Ticonderoga. But by 1759, the tide had turned in favor of the British, with the capture of Fortress Louisbourg and Forts Duquesne and Frontenac.

This battle was not very large, either in men involved or area. The total forces of both sides did not exceed five hundred men. The actual battle area probably did not exceed one-half mile. The battle itself did not prolong the war, nor hasten its end. Its outcome did not give any advantage to either side in future clashes.

But what a battle it was! It was fought primarily by native-born settlers of New England against native-born Canadians and their Indian allies of New France. It pitted the best of the English Rangers, led by Robert Rogers, against the best of the French Canadians and Indians, led by the partisan Langy. It was fought in the rugged mountain wilderness that we know today as the Adirondacks. The rocky, snow-covered, thickly forested hills were as cruel and remorseless as the antagonists who fought to the death on the slopes.

The battle did not end in a draw. It was a clear-cut victory for the French and Indians, and resulted in the almost total annihilation of the English Rangers. Only darkness saved Robert Rogers and the pitiful remnants of his force. It was known then and is still known today as...

"THE BATTLE ON SNOWSHOES."

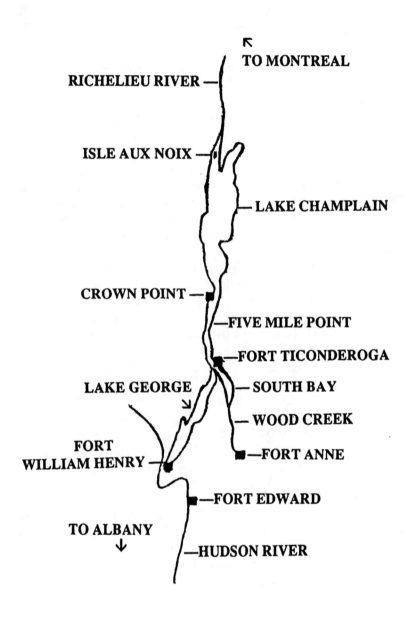

TO MONTREAL

RICHELIEU RIVER —

ISLE AUX NOIX —

— LAKE CHAMPLAIN

CROWN POINT —

— FIVE MILE POINT

— FORT TICONDEROGA

LAKE GEORGE — SOUTH BAY

— WOOD CREEK

FORT
WILLIAM HENRY — — FORT ANNE

— FORT EDWARD

TO ALBANY

— HUDSON RIVER

MAP I. THE CHAMPLAIN VALLEY

1. THE ANTAGONISTS ───────────────────

IT should not have taken England and her American colonies almost seven years of fighting to defeat New France. They possessed almost every advantage imaginable.

The British navy, mightiest in the world, controlled the seas and effectively strangled Canada's lifeline from France. Supplies and re-inforcements from France were reduced to "slim and none." Years of back-to-back crop failures, coupled with the thievery and corruption of the Canadian leaders Francois Bigot (intendant of Canada), Hugues Péan (town major of Quebec), and Joseph Cadet (commissary general), had the population starving, weakened, and discouraged. (Hamilton, pp. 129-130; Rutledge, pp. 468-469.) Canada was in dire straits, and there would be no relief.

The entire population of Canada in the 1750's is believed to have been about 60,000. In comparison, the New England colony of Rhode Island alone had well over 40,000. The British and Americans outnumbered the French and Canadians by a ratio of more than twenty to one. (Hamilton, p. 133.)

New France also had an enormous territory to defend, thus spreading her pitifully thin forces even further. Fortress Louisbourg, on Cape Breton Island, Nova Scotia, held the easternmost sentinel at the edge of the Atlantic Ocean. The cities of Quebec, Three Rivers, and Montreal guarded the St. Lawrence River Valley. Fort Carillon (Ticonderoga) and Fort St. Frederic (Crown Point) on the shores of Lake Champlain, were connected to the St. Lawrence by a series of forts and villages along the Richelieu River. The Great Lakes were guarded by Forts Niagara, Frontenac, Venango, Presque Isle, Le Boeuf, Duquesne, Detroit, and Michilimackinaw. The great rivers of the interior were defended by Kaskaskia, St. Famille, Fort De Chartres, and others, all the way to New Orleans.

In contrast to Canada, the American colonies were blessed with better soil and longer growing seasons. They could start the campaign seasons sooner and outwait the French when withdrawing into winter quarters. They also had the luxury of ice-free seaports to receive the necessary mountains of supplies and troops all year long. (Hamilton, pp. 19-20.) They had more men, more supplies, more regular troops, more *everything*. So how did the French "David" stave off the English "Goliath" for all those years? Basically, it came down to three things.

First: Unity. Canada was a feudalistic system like her mother country, France, and its leadership was absolute in its powers. When the country went to war, the commands were unquestioned, total, and absolute. There was no arguing or bickering over troops, strategy, or commands, such as was found in the American colonies. New France's orders were carried out quickly and decisively. (Hamilton, pp. 125-126.)

Second: The fighting spirit and experience of the French and Canadian troops. The "Troupes de Terre" that arrived with General Dieskau and the Marquis de Montcalm were professional soldiers—combat-hardened veterans of the wars in Europe, experienced in battle tactics such as siege warfare. The Canadians were masters of the forests. They had fought for their very existence since the days of Champlain against the hated Iroquois, and later against the English. The men of Canada not only learned from the Indians the art of warfare in the forest both in summer and winter, but eventually surpassed and excelled them at it. From father to son, from generation to generation, evolved a fighting man impervious to weather and hardships, superior in marksmanship, and a master of ambushes and raids.

Finally: Leadership. The French officers were men who had courage, experience, and initiative. Just as cream rises to the top, so did men with the qualities of leadership and bravery such as Dumas, La Corne, Marin, and Langy. They were descended from generations of fighting families. This was their glass of wine. Superior British numbers meant only one thing to them: more targets to shoot, more scalps to take.

2. WEATHER _____

WINTER weather in the Adirondacks can be brutally cold. In 1757, Bougainville recorded the daily temperature in his journal as he traveled between Quebec, Montreal, and the Lake Champlain battle front. The average temperature he recorded for January of that year was about 6 degrees Fahrenheit. Compare that to the average mean temperature of January 1995, which was 31.3 degrees Fahrenheit. We know from accounts of the Battle that Lake George was frozen over, and three to four feet of snow covered the ground. We can only imagine how factors such as wind chill, darkness, and precipitation intensified the cold.

During severe winters, snow levels might measure three to five feet in February. Lakes froze solidly, and even rivers as large as the St. Lawrence and the Hudson froze over. Up until the 1900's, cutting blocks of ice was an important winter business.

This is not to say that it was always cold and frozen; they had January and spring thaws back then also. On January 3, 1758, the weather thawed to such an extent that the melting snow and ice caused the Hudson River to rise, flooding most of the huts on Rogers Island at Fort Edward, destroying much firewood and many hundreds of pairs of snowshoes the Rangers had laboriously made. (Loescher, 1946, pp. 233.) However, five days later the temperature dropped sharply, and everything froze solid again.

People today often wonder how difficult life must have been back in those days. Basically, people were toughened to the elements. They did not have central heating and air conditioning that we take for granted today. Their bodies attuned themselves to the rugged lifestyles they lived and the physical work that all men, women, and children performed daily. Also, back in those days, only the strong survived nature's weeding processes of disease, disabilities, wars, famines, and accidents. Whatever was done, even the act of getting from one place to another, was done by walking, paddling a canoe, or saddling a horse and riding. It was a physically demanding lifestyle, with few "creature comforts."

Finally, they knew how to dress warmly in layers of wool, furs, and animal skins. Even when wet, these materials would hold the warmth better than most of the synthetic fabrics we wear today. Our rugged ancestors also knew how to sleep in the woods at night in the dead of winter, without freezing. They would clear out a circle with their snowshoes, banking the snow up into a wall around them. Thus sheltered from the wind, they would build a fire in the middle of the circle. Lying close together upon a "mattress" of spruce and hemlock boughs piled three to six inches deep, they could pass the night in relative comfort. What we do warily, once in a while and as an adventure, they did daily and never gave it a second thought. Much of this knowledge of how to survive in the woods has been lost through the passing of years.

3. TERRAIN ───────────────────

IT has been said that long ago, on October 2, 1536, Jacques Cartier was led to the top of a mountain behind the Indian village of Hochelaga on the St. Lawrence River. The huge hill he climbed upon was later to be called Mont Royal, and if the day was crisp and clear, Jacques Cartier would have been the first white man ever to see the Adirondack Mountains of New York lying to the south. (White, p. 3.)

Several generations later, three Frenchmen, led by Samuel de Champlain, would be the first white men to have actually penetrated into the mountains by the huge lake that he named after himself, Lac Champlain. Accompanying his Algonquin Indian allies as far south as the rocky promontory that we know today as Ticonderoga, Champlain and his men helped defeat a huge force of Iroquois in a fierce battle. This encounter in July 1609, marked the one of the first recorded uses of firearms against the Indians.

The third recorded sighting of the Adirondacks by a white man was that of the French Jesuit martyr Father Isaac Jogues on his way into captivity and subsequent death at the hands of the Iroquois. Reaching the sparkling blue body of water that we know today as Lake George (Jamieson, p. 13), Father Jogues christened it then, "Lac Du Saint Sacrement," because that day was the feast of Corpus Christi. (Loescher, 1946, p. 406.) Thus do we have the French explorers and missionaries being the first white men to see and penetrate the mountains.

The Adirondacks are some of the oldest mountains in the world, dating back almost three billion years. The peaks once exceeded heights of more than 20,000 feet, but through the ice ages the movements of the glaciers eroded them down to what we have today. Presently there are two peaks over 5000 feet in height, and 44 peaks over 4000 feet in height. (White, pp. 10-11.)

The ice ages and movements of glaciers also caused the rivers, lakes, and ponds to be formed. Lake George is a spring-fed lake, 32 miles long and almost four miles across at its widest point. It lies 321 feet above sea level and drops 225 feet into Lake Champlain, which flows northward into the St. Lawrence River, emptying into the Atlantic Ocean. Only twelve miles to the west of Lake George are Glens Falls and Fort Edward, situated on the Hudson River, which flows southward and empties into the Atlantic at New York City. (Hamilton, pp. 15-16.)

The Iroquois called Lake George "Andiatoracte," meaning "where the lake shuts itself." The boiling river that empties from Lake George into Lake Champlain was called La Chute, and remains so to this day.

A map drawn in 1756 labeled the Adirondacks as "Couchsacraga," an Indian term that meant "beaver hunting country." The area was also known as the Dismal Wilderness and the Great Northern Woods. (White, pp. 50-51; Jamieson, pp. 1-3.) It was thickly forested, uncharted, virgin wilderness that was relatively unknown, even well into the 1800's. The source of the Columbia River was discovered sixty years before the source of the Hudson was. (White, p. 5.) Today the Adirondack Park covers over six million acres, the largest park east of the Mississippi.

Neither the Iroquois, who lived south and west of the Adirondacks, nor the Algonquin tribes, who lived to the north and in Canada, ever settled in the Adirondack Mountains. Both tribes used them for hunting, trapping, and fishing. When these two enemies met, it usually ended in bloodshed. The Adirondacks formed a boundary that marked a difference of lifestyles for the two Indian tribes. The Indians of the north were primarily hunters and gatherers, so in hard winters of poor hunting, famine would arise and the people would be forced to eat anything, even the inner barks of certain trees to survive. The Iroquois, to the south, not only had game in abundance, but rich fertile country on which they farmed crops of corn, beans, squash, and pumpkins to sustain them throughout the seasons. Thus, the derogatory Iroquois word, "Adirondacks," meaning, "those who eat trees" or "Barkeaters," was applied to the Algonquins and later to the mountains in which they hunted and died. (White, p. 52; Smith, p. 13.)

In some respects, the land of the Adirondacks has changed, while in others, it has not. The Indian paths and trails of yesteryear have become the roads and highways of today. Deserted, forested shores now have summer camps and year round homes lining them. The southern end of Lake George is dominated by the bustling village of the same name, with its motels, restaurants, fast food stands, and amusement park rides. But right amid all the twentieth-century hubbub and confusion, stands the re-built wooden replica of Fort William Henry. At the northern end of the lake stands the sprawling village of Ticonderoga, but if you follow the waters of the lake as they wind and cascade down the falls of La Chute River, you will still come under the guns of Fort Carillon, now known as Fort Ticonderoga. Both forts are open to the public, both have uniformed guides, exhibits and museums, and both serve to educate the public of an area and an era steeped in history. On the last weekend of June each year, Fort Ticonderoga hosts the "Grande Encampment," which brings together French, British, and Indian re-enactors by the hundreds. Camp life at the fort is acted out as it was 240 years ago, with men and women going about their daily tasks. Food is prepared in the eighteenth-century manner. Muskets and equipment are cleaned and readied, leather craftsmen make moccasins and shoes, and traders still hawk their goods. Indian councils and mock battles are re-enacted, complete with the thunder of musketry, the roar of cannon, and the wailing of bagpipes, turning back the clock of time to the French and Indian War. History is re-born for the visitors and tourists.

In 1979, I started a French and Indian War event that has grown from period hunting and camping, to a full-scale re-creation of the life of eighteenth-century forest scouts. Today almost seventy re-enactors of both French and British forces gather in October for a week of friendly combat against one another. Whaleboats and bateaux sail upon the lake; birchbark canoes silently glide across the surface while their paddlers warily avoid one another. In the woods, men of both sides scout, camp, and set ambushes for the opposing force. All clothing, foods, and accoutrements are strictly eighteenth-century. Held in the huge wilderness area on the east side of Lake George, it is as close as one can get to the true experience.

The lake itself today is still spring-fed, cold, and treacherous. A storm or stiff wind can whip the blue waters into a boiling cauldron, forcing a canoe into the safety of the shore to avoid being overturned or swamped. Winter brings other dangers. Being such a large body of water, Lake George does not freeze over in one solid, smooth piece. Rather, different sections freeze separately, then come together in force, creating pressure ridges. Depending on the winter and its coldness, there can be as many as twenty or as few as eight ridges. When crossing these ridges one must exercise extreme caution not to fall through the weaker ice on the lee side underneath the ledges.

When I was about to trek the lake in February 1990, I contacted my good friend Ed Murphy, Glens Falls fireman and longtime Lake George fishing guide. Ed showed me the best routes of travel, how to cross the pressure ridges, and what spots to avoid. Ice is thicker on the southern end by Fort William Henry, with thicknesses some years of thirty inches. The northern end freezes later and averages around sixteen inches in thickness. Today's travel on the lake is made much more dangerous by machines which the owners of many homes and summer camps place in the water to keep their docks and boat launches free from the crush of the ice pack. These machines are propeller devices which create a tremendous current of water that swirls out and around the docks. Sometimes the force of these machines can push a strong current of water into the lake hundreds of feet from shore. If you were walking along the ice and came upon an area affected by one of these machines, the thickness of the ice beneath you might be reduced from twenty-two inches, to sixteen inches, to four inches, and down to two inches, all within a distance of less than one hundred yards. It is not something to be taken lightly.

4. THE FORTS

FRONTIER FORTS varied in size and construction. Some were simple stockades of upright logs, sharpened at the top, placed close together. Other forts were made of horizontal log cribbing with earth and stone packed between the walls. Still others were elaborately made of mortar and stone. Some had blockhouses, watch towers, redoubts, demi-lunes, and glacis, while others did not. (Hamilton, pp. 92-93.) But every fort was created and used for a definite purpose: to resist attack from a hostile enemy force. The bigger and stronger the attacking force, the bigger and stronger the fort and its emplacements had to be.

There was a limit to every fort's defense capability, of course. The greatest military engineer of the eighteenth century, French strategist Sebastien le Prestre Vauban, admitted that no matter how strong a fortress was, it could and would eventually be taken by a superior, determined force. An army of, say 15,000 to 20,000 men with heavy siege artillery, good engineers and sappers, plenty of food and provisions, and enough time, would topple any fort in the New World. (Hamilton, p. 155.) The biggest problem was getting to the fort. Roads had to be hacked and carved over mountains, swamps, and through impenetrable forests, so that the siege artillery could be brought to bear on the fort. Without the employment of artillery, chances of successfully assaulting a fort were very poor. Adding to the hardship of physically moving these huge guns were the problems of heat, rains, disease, lack of nourishing foods and, of course, the constant threat of ambushes and raids by enemy forces. It made for a truly slow, tedious, and immense undertaking.

The only other alternative was to move by water, if possible; most times a considerably smoother, quicker, and easier mode of travel. The problem with that, was that most enemy forts were built on places that denied passage by water. The forts in the Hudson River and Lake Champlain regions all fit into this category. Let's look at the British and French forts that figure predominantly in the events that led up to the Battle on Snowshoes.

Fort Edward was an irregularly shaped, three-bastioned fort, built of horizontal log cribbing. It was situated at the end of the navigable water in the upper Hudson River, known as "the great carrying place." (Cuneo, p. 20.) For years, a trader named Lydius ran a trading post there; it was burned and later rebuilt. In 1755 construction began on the fort that was briefly named Fort Lyman, after Col. Phineas Lyman, who was in charge of building the fort, and who was second in command of the army under Sir William Johnson. The name was later changed to Fort Edward, in honor of Edward Augustus, Duke of York. (Stott, p. 6.) As the war progressed, Fort Edward's defenses were enlarged to accommodate the huge numbers of arriving troops, and it eventually became the main staging area for British army operations.

On an island immediately across from the fort, a hospital was constructed where the Rangers set up their encampment, living together in huts. (Cuneo, p. 43.) It became known as "Rogers Island." It was from here that Rogers led his 181 men north on that fateful day in March of 1758.

Fort William Henry was the farthest British outpost in the early years of the war. It was built in the autumn of 1755, following the Battle of Lake George, by the orders of Sir William Johnson. It was also there that Sir William re-named Lac St. Sacrement. "I have given it the name, Lake George," said Johnson, "not only in honor of His Majesty (George II), but to ascertain his undoubted dominion here." (Loescher, 1946, p. 406.) The fort was built a few hundred yards west of the September battle area, and, like Fort Edward, was made out of horizontal log cribbing filled with earth and stones. (Steele, pp. 58-59.) It was attacked in March, 1757, by a force of 1500 French and Indians, led by Rigaud de Vaudreuil, brother of the Canadian governor. Losing the element of surprise, the French force could not take the fort due to lack of artillery. After burning many of the outbuildings and boats, the French made their way back to Canada. (Hamilton, p. 196; Bird, pp. 145-157.) In August, 1757, the French forces under Montcalm advanced by land and water, and lay siege to the fort for over a week. Following its surrender, they leveled it, leaving behind nothing but a pile of smoldering ashes.

Fort St. Frederic, on La Pointe de Chevelure, or Scalp Point, was built by the French in 1731. (Hamilton, p. 212.) It was a strong, square fort made of stone. It had three regular bastions, topped by round sentry boxes and a citadel in an irregular bastion. The citadel itself was octagonal in shape and was four stories high with a round, sloping roof. It had six chimneys and stood in the northwest corner of the fortress, where entry was gained by a drawbridge over a small ditch. Also inside were the stone barracks, chapel, storehouses, and other buildings. During the campaign seasons, the open plain south of the fort was the site of temporary camps of tents and huts, accommodating large numbers of men. Fort St. Frederic was not as big as Carillon, but it was the dominating fort in the Champlain Valley for over twenty years. It was from there that the raids of 1745 and 1747 were launched against Saratoga, Fort Clinton, Fort Massachusetts, and others.

After the battle on the Monongahela and Braddock's subsequent defeat in 1755, the campaign papers that were carried by Braddock were captured and forwarded to Governor Vaudreuil at Quebec. (Lancaster, p. 24.) It was then that Canada first learned of the proposed attack on Fort St. Frederic by Sir William Johnson and his provincial forces. Consequently, Baron Ludwig von Dieskau, the French military commander recently sent to New France, was dispatched to stop this invasion with a force of 216 French regulars, 684 Canadians, and about 600 Indians.

After their defeat at the Battle of Lake George, the survivors of Dieskau's force retreated northward. Stopping at the site of present-day Fort Ticonderoga, they immediately commenced construction of a fort that was designed by the Canadian engineer, Lotbiniere. It was called "Carillon" by the French, and it became one of the most famous forts in the history of North America. (Lancaster, pp. 36-38; Hamilton, p. 169.)

Fort Carillon, or Ticonderoga as it was later named by the British, was THE strongest of all the forts in the New York theater of the war. Originally built of oaks in 1755, it was later re-built with thick stone walls, demi-lunes, redoubts, and barracks. It had its own bakery, gardens, and hospital. Below the fort sprawled a huge settlement that could accommodate the immense numbers of French and their Indian allies that encamped during the summer campaign seasons. It was at this fort that Robert Rogers scouted, ambushed, and captured French soldiers. It was also from this fort that the French gave Rogers his first taste of defeat, in the "first" (January, 1757) battle on snowshoes, after he had captured the provision sleighs going from

Carillon to Fort St. Frederic. This was also the scene of one of Rogers' notorious pranks. He and his men, unable to breach the defenses of the fort, instead slaughtered the oxen and cattle outside the walls. On one of the dead beasts' horns, he left an "I.O.U." receipt, so that the French would have no doubt as to who committed the deed. From this same fort, Captain d'Hebecourt sent Langy to collect on that receipt, on March 13, 1758.

There are many people who believe that the French at Carillon were warned of Rogers' coming, either by the prisoner (a servant of Mr. Best, the sutler) taken by Langy on March 6, or John Robens, who deserted or disappeared from Israel Putnam's scouting party on February 27. (Loescher, 1946, pp. 237-237.)

What does that mean, "They were warned"? Let's break this down with some common sense. First, if the French "knew" when Rogers was coming (i.e., 9:00 A.M. on March 13), where he was going (i.e., the west demi-lune), and which route he was coming from (i.e., up the falls road past the sawmill), they would have prepared an ambush that no one would have survived. But they obviously did not. They may have heard that a scout was to be sent against them, but so what? This was nothing new. This was the third year of the war, and scouts, raids, and ambushes were an everyday fact of life. Without particulars, it meant nothing. There is nothing in any French reports or documents that suggests their knowledge.

In the early years of the war, the French and their Indian allies were always on the offensive, striking south and east in hit-and-run raids. When Rogers started scouting for Sir William Johnson in September, 1755, he was the first successful long-range scout that the British had in their employ. His early ambushes and raids were extremely successful because of one more thing, the element of surprise. The French never expected the timid English to leave their forts and become so bold in the forests; they were caught off guard for a while. As the years went on and Rogers' Rangers continued their raids, the French tightened their security. It was no surprise to either side in 1758 that the enemy constantly had raiders afoot.

The French at Carillon did not know of Rogers' Rangers' objective or, more importantly, the route the Rangers would take. The Adirondacks are a vast wilderness area, and the English could attack from any number of directions. But most important to the scrutiny of modern-day researchers and historians is this simple fact: Rogers himself did not decide the route of travel into the Trout Brook Valley until the very morning of March 13. (Loescher, 1946, p. 245; Cuneo, p. 76.)

It was only by happenstance, or fate if you will, that his tracks were discovered by the Abenakis. The reason that many of history's battles were fought where they were is due to happenstance; opportunity. Like Braddock's defeat on the Monongahela, like the Civil War Battle of Gettysburg; the location of the Battle on Snowshoes was not planned ahead of time. It happened simply as the two forces met each other unexpectedly, and escalated from there into the battle.

5. WEAPONS,
EQUIPMENT AND PROVISIONS

THE weapons and equipment used in the battle were as diverse as the men who carried them. It is too easy, and indeed inaccurate, to say that the Rangers all carried "Brown Bess" muskets, while the French troops were all armed with the 1728 army model. For the sake of clarity, let's divide the participants into three groups of Rangers, Indians, and French.

RANGERS: In 1755 Robert Rogers led fifty men from New Hampshire to Lake George, where Fort William Henry was to be built. Rogers and his men brought with them their own personal firelocks, probably New England fowlers; plain, simple, smoothbore muskets that they used for hunting and for defending their homes. One or more of these men could have carried a double-barreled fowler. Although not as common as the French double gun, it was available to individuals. (Gallup and Shaffer, pp. 92-93.)

Captain Hobbs' and Captain Speakman's companies were a makeshift lot. (Hobbs, the famous fighting deacon from New Hampshire, died of smallpox in an Albany hospital, in January, 1757. He was replaced by Captain Bulkeley, who was killed in the Battle on Snowshoes. Speakman was killed in action in January, 1757, at the French ambush of Rogers' Rangers, see pp. 31-32. He was replaced by Captain Stark.) Some of the men were from the Boston waterfront, including Irish Catholics, sailors, and Spaniards. (Cuneo, p. 42; Loescher, 1946, p. 101.) It is entirely possible that a blunderbuss or a coach gun could have been brought along by a former sailor or buccaneer. Regulation Brown Bess muskets were made available in 1756, and some men immediately set to cutting down the 46" barrels to 38" for ease and quickness of handling in the woods. Excavations on Rogers Island in New York State have turned up many cut-off pieces of barrels, eight inches in length. (Stott, p. 25.) Officers such as Rogers, Stark, or Bulkeley, may have purchased a short officer's carbine, smaller and lighter than the Brown Bess, and these officers also may have carried a pistol along with them. All

1. Rangers with Arms and Equipment

Rangers would have carried edged weapons such as knives, tomahawks, and bayonets. Perhaps a cutlass or short sword may have been employed, but this is doubtful considering the awkwardness of carrying it in the bush.

On the Ranger's body was a powder horn slung over the shoulder and resting on the right side, while a leather sling holding the bayonet and tomahawk rested on his left side. A canteen made of wood hung at his left side by a strap that passed over his left shoulder. It contained four days' ration of rum (about four gills) which was mixed with water and known as "grog." Around his waist on a leather belt hung a bag made of leather or sealskin, which contained sixty lead balls and a few hundred smaller balls the size of peas, known as buckshot. Sometimes they would shoot these together. (Cuneo, p. 53.)

Tricorne hats were worn on the parade grounds, but in the brush the "Scotch bonnets" were highly favored. Those who could not get them wore round felt hats cropped close, or raccoon or bearskin fur hats. Early Rangers were clothed in homespun, wools, and buckskin hunting shirts and leggings. Hobbs' and Speakman's companies were later dressed in a "cloth of soft grey duffle" to give them a more uniform appearance. (Loescher, 1946, p. 278.) Rogers' own company was issued green uniforms in January 1758, and probably a good portion of the Rangers in the snowshoe battle were wearing these. The outer coats were described as short jackets without sleeves, whose armholes and shoulders were strengthened by wings, similar to those of the Grenadiers. Underneath was a green waistcoat whose sleeves passed through the outer garment. Both were lined with green serge and contrasted against the coarse woolen "frieze." White metal buttons were on the front and cuffs, while officers' coats were lined with a silver lace trim. (Loescher, 1946, pp. 280-281.) Breeches made of wool, deerskin, or canvas extended to the knees; while leggings of wool, deerskin, or canvas reached from above the Rangers' knees to their ankles, and were tied at the ankle and knee by garters. Packs or haversacks were carried on the Ranger's back on the left side and would contain his food rations, personal items, ice skates, and ice creepers. (Ice creepers could be attached with leather thongs to the bottom of shoes, moccasins, or snowshoes. They were flat bars of metal with sharp prongs sticking out, for better traction on the ice.) Blankets were rolled, tied, and slung over the shoulder, and snowshoes would be carried

2. Indians with Arms and Equipment

the same way when not being used. Mittens were a necessary item that all men needed to have in the cold winter weather of the Adirondacks. Most men attached them with a leather thong, either passed around the neck or tied onto the cuffs of the coat.

INDIANS: The Indians would also have been armed with a variety of weapons, primarily trade guns of British, French, or Belgian manufacture. These relatively cheaply made guns were remarkably similar to one another, with characteristics of short barrels, smaller calibers, and enlarged trigger guards that allowed two or three fingers to be inserted, thus enabling a man to fire the weapon without having to take off his mittens. Some Indians may have acquired the superior Tulle *fusil de chasse*. Others may have been armed with older relics of guns from earlier wars such as the English dog-lock musket. (Gallup and Shaffer, p. 90.)

Remember, Indians were not issued arms per se by either the French or English. Occasionally the gift of a musket to a chief or a prominent warrior would be made in recognition of bravery, loyalty, or just good politics. Most Indians came by their weapons by trading furs, skins, or crafts such as moccasins. Occasionally they would pick them up at a battle, raid, or ambush, from the body of a soldier or an unlucky farmer. Until Indian warriors were able to obtain weapons of their own, they (especially the younger ones) used bows and arrows. There are accounts of these being used at the siege of Fort William Henry in 1757, and through the following wars of Pontiac's Rebellion and even into the American Revolution. Indians also excelled at hand-to-hand combat, where they could rush upon a foe and slam a tomahawk, war club, or knife into his body. Both the French and English made edged weapons of knives and tomahawks easily available to their Indian allies; they were staples of forest warfare.

Indians dressed very lightly, even during the coldest weather. It is not uncommon to read of "Savages stripped to the waist, smeared with vermilion paint and coats of bear grease." Most Indians carried blankets and wore shirts, woolen breechclouts, and leggings made of deerskins or wool. Many heads were bare, save for scalplocks and ornaments, while some wore hats made of fur. Many had taken their woolen blankets and fashioned them into blanket coats, which were extremely warm even when wet with rain or snow. All wore moccasins of elk, moose, or deerskin leather, well greased and lined with shredded birchbark or hollow

3. French Marines with Arms and Equipment

deer hair for insulation and warmth. The snowshoes they used were handmade and ranged in style from the long, slender, "pickerel" type of the Crees, to the beavertail or bear paw types of the Abenakis and Algonquins.

FRENCH: The French force was composed of essentially three different groups of men: The volunteers of the La Reine regiment; the Compagnie Franche, or Colony Marines; and Langy's Canadians, who were probably *Milice* (Canadian militia).

The men of La Reine and Compagnie Franche would be very similarly dressed as soldiers. A long linen shirt or *chemise* reached almost to the knees. This was tucked into woolen breeches (*les culottes*) lined with linen. Woolen socks or stockings (*les bas*) would be covered by either the issue canvas gaiters, or woolen leggings (*mitasses*), and worn inside high moccasins (*bottes sauvages*). The neck would be covered by a linen stock (*la cravat*) or a scarf of silk or wool. The waistcoat (*la veste*) of wool would be next followed by the *justacorps*, or great uniform outer coat of white wool. The justacorps had turned-back gauntlet cuffs of contrasting colors (blue for marines, red for La Reine), with metal buttons. On their heads the men could have worn the issue tricorne hat (*le chapeau*) with a silk or woolen scarf underneath for warmth, or a fatigue cap (*bonnet du police*) made of the same cloth as their coats. (Gallup and Shaffer, pp. 56-83.) The soldiers of La Reine most likely would have carried the 1746 army musket, while the Marines probably had the 1717 or 1728 marine musket, or the 1734 grenadier musket. Over each marine's shoulder and resting on his right side was a leather shooting bag, called *la giberne*. Attached to this was a leather powder flask called *la fourniment*. On his left side hung a leather belt with a double "frog," which was to hold the bayonet and tomahawk. Inside the *giberne* would have been extra flints, hammer stalls and vent picks and perhaps a screwdriver, and almost thirty rolled paper cartridges. (Gallup and Shaffer, pp. 94-104.)

The Canadians under Langy wore linen and woolen shirts, woolen breeches, or perhaps a woolen breechclout (*breyette*) and leggings. Most surely they wore woolen socks and stockings inside their *bottes sauvage*. On their heads they preferred woolen caps (*tuques*) of red, blue, or white, or woolen caps edged and lined with fur, commonly called "Canadian caps." Over all was worn a *capot* of wool in different colors of gray, white, blue, or brown. It should be noted that a *capot* or *capote*, and a blanket coat are different but have similarities. A *capot* is a well-tailored coat of civilian attire, complete with turned-back cuffs and buttons, pleated, and very similar in style to that of the military *justacorps*. There was a single button at the neck, and the waist was gathered by use of a woven sash, called a *ceinture fleche*. *Capots* were also made with an attached hood. (Gallup and Shaffer, pp. 73-83.) Not to be forgotten were the snowshoes. The Canadians, having been brought up since childhood on snowshoes, were masters at that mode of travel, literally being able to run on them without tripping or falling. All French and Canadians probably would have carried metal ice creepers in their packs. (Gallup and Shaffer, p. 129.)

Lastly, officers such as Langy, Richerville, and Durantaye would have worn a *gorget* at their throat. Symbol of rank, and last vestige of armor, it was worn whether dressed in the justacorps, capot, or on the bare chest, as did Captain Daniel de Beaujeu at the ambush of Braddock's army in 1755.

PROVISIONS: Provisions were carried in knapsacks or haversacks, and sometimes extra gear was pulled on toboggans or hand sleighs. Most people today think that the frontier diet of scouts and woodsmen was parched corn, jerky, and nothing else. Although these foods, along with pemmican, were the staples, a great many other foodstuffs were available for the packs of the forest fighters. Dried rice, peas, barley, rolled oats, and corn meal could be boiled in water, and pieces of dried beef, venison, or moose could be added. Sausages, bread, and cheese were carried, and flour could be used to make breads and journey cakes along the trail. Salt was available, as were maple and brown sugars. Ginger, tea, and cakes of chocolate could be brewed in hot water for drinks. Officers such as Langy might have carried a small metal flask of brandy or wine. Individual items in packs could include combs, soap, razors, sewing needles and awls, pipes, and tobacco. Every man carried means of making fire with the flint and steel wherever he traveled. Small pieces of candle, perhaps a spoon carved from wood, and a small clasp knife would have found their way into many of the men's packs. Canadians were especially fond of knives (*couteaux*), often carrying three of them when in the woods. (Gallup and Shaffer, pp. 124-126.) Extra items that might have been pulled on the sleighs included canvas tarps, extra blankets, food, and kettles for cooking.

I believe that two of the determining factors in the outcome of the battle were the arms used by the French and the superior marksmanship of the Canadians. Indeed, most of the 650 casualties of the British during the battle for Quebec on the Plains of Abraham were inflicted both before and after the climax of the battle by the Canadian sharpshooters. Before this battle, Wolfe's failed attempt at Montmorency in July, 1759, was due in part by the devastating fire poured down upon the British from the heights, particularly that of the Canadians from Montreal. One French officer of the time described the Canadians: "They make war only by swift attacks and almost always by success against the English who are not as vigorous, nor as adroit in the use of firearms as they, nor as practiced in forest warfare." (Eccles, p. 89.) The Swedish naturalist Peter Kalm stated in his journals in 1749, "I have seldom seen any people shoot with such dexterity as these.... There was scarcely one of them who was not a clever marksman and who did not own a rifle." (Kalm, p. 563.) These men of the North literally grew up with firearms in their hands for use in hunting and fighting the Iroquois from the earliest days of New France. They were seldom, if ever, without their trusted fusils in their hands.

The structure and design of the French fusils, especially that of the *de chasse* was very similar to that of the later Pennsylvania and Kentucky rifles. Long, with a curved, dropped stock, it lent itself better to accurate, aimed fire. The lighter and smaller lead ball had a slightly straighter and flatter trajectory than that of the Brown Bess. The Bess, and later the 1763 French Charleville, were not intended for individual aimed fire, but rather, were created for speeded volley fire from ranks of massed infantry. They are a more awkward weapon to shoot with consistent accuracy. This is not to suggest that they cannot hit where aimed, or that marksmanship cannot be attained. On the contrary, a few modern-day New England Rangers, Fred Gowen, and Mark and Paul Daiute, are excellent shots with their "Besses" at local shoots and competitions. But we are talking about exceptions here, rather than the rule.

Finally, the use of buckshot, which has its advantage in close combat and ambushes, loses its effectiveness and hitting power over increased distances. When the Rangers and French fired at each other over a considerable distance, the advantage was definitely with the Canadians.

4. French Partisan Leaders, left to right: Richerville, Langy, Durantaye

6. THE LEADERS _____

LANGY and Rogers were the opposing leaders in the Battle on Snowshoes. They were the ones who called the moves and countermoves. They were on the spot and in charge. Their decisions and leadership determined the battle and its outcome.

Comparing the two is difficult. Let's see how they match up.

PHYSICALLY - Rogers has been described as big and imposing, standing over six feet in height, having slender legs and a thick upper body. His face was described as having gray eyes, thick lips, and a large protruding nose. He was also said to be strong, athletic, and a local wrestling champion. (Cuneo, p. 12.)

There are no records describing Langy's appearance. I can only see Langy as a typical male of eighteenth-century Canada, probably 5' 7" to 5' 9" in height, about 150 to 170 pounds, dark hair, green or brown eyes and, like Rogers, a strong, athletic build.

AGE AND MILITARY EXPERIENCE - Give this important edge to Langy. He was born in October, 1723, and Rogers was born in November, 1731. At the time of the Battle on Snowshoes Langy would have been 34 years old, while Rogers would have been 26. Langy came from a military family, had served as a cadet in the marines since the late 1740's, making ensign second in 1748, and ensign first in 1751. Rogers' military career started when he was fourteen years old, like many other youths of his day in New England, serving in a local militia company. In 1755 he procured a provincial captaincy for recruiting a company of men. In 1756 he received a British commission appointing him as captain of "An Independent Company of Rangers." Langy, on the other hand, had the years of experience raiding on the frontiers. He also had an edge on Rogers by having participated in such major battles as the sieges of Fort Beausejour, Fort Oswego, and Fort William Henry.

Now, let's review the careers of these two remarkable leaders.

THE LEADERS:
ROGERS

ROBERT ROGERS was born in Methuen, Massachusetts, on November 18, 1731, of Scotch immigrants from Northern Ireland. (Cuneo, p. 4.)

When he was only eight years old, his family left Methuen and moved to a tract of farmland some ten miles from Rumford, New Hampshire, which was the nearest community. (Cuneo, p. 6.) There he grew up learning the ways of the farm, and also the ways of the woods. As a lad of fourteen he served in a local militia company, and the next summer he joined another under the command of a Captain Eastman. (Cuneo, p. 8.) When King George's War ended in 1748, Rogers gave up the idea of farming, which he did not care for, and spent much of his time in the woods and mountains of northern New Hampshire, where he made the acquaintance of several Indians and Indian traders. It is rumored that he was engaged in the smuggling trade, a practice not uncommon in those days.

In 1753 he was part of a group of twenty men authorized by the New Hampshire assembly to survey and mark out a road to the Coos Meadows on the Connecticut River. In 1754 the Indians started a series of small raids along the frontier, prompting the governor to call out the militia again. Rogers served with a Lieutenant Goffe and patrolled the lands between the Merrimack and Contoocook Rivers. (Cuneo, p. 11.) In September, the raids slackened and he was discharged. Later that same fall, Rogers got involved in a scheme with some notorious counterfeiters. In January, 1755, the authorities in Portsmouth issued warrants for the arrest of nineteen suspects. Robert Rogers was one of them. (Cuneo, pp. 14-15.)

One of the earliest known existing manuscripts in Rogers' handwriting is a note he penned to a certain Carty Gilman, a man to whom he had passed counterfeit notes. He pleaded with Gilman to destroy the evidence, "For why should such an honest man be killed." (Loescher, 1946, pp. 19-21.) Gilman was still in possession of Rogers' letter when the sheriffs came to investigate the matter. Gilman tried to destroy the letter by shoving it in his mouth to swallow it. He did not succeed, and it remains to this day Rogers' first recorded letter. Because of lack of concrete evidence, Rogers was not convicted. He literally escaped by the skin of his teeth.

After this unnerving brush with the law, opportunity knocked at Rogers' door. In February, 1755, Massachusetts was raising recruits for a campaign against the French in Nova Scotia, and Rogers saw this as a chance for redemption. He contacted a Major Joseph Frye and offered to enlist men for the campaign. Major Frye advanced him money, and Rogers recruited men from New Hampshire, bringing them to Portsmouth. (Cuneo, p. 17.) While there, Rogers learned that the New Hampshire governor, Benning Wentworth, was looking to raise a New Hampshire regiment to go against the French at Fort St. Frederic. Not above double-dealing, Rogers then proceeded to ingratiate himself with Wentworth. He secured a captain's commission, and promptly turned over the recruits in Portsmouth to the New Hampshire regiment under Colonel Blanchard. (Cuneo, p. 18; Loescher, 1946, pp. 20-21.)

When Major Frye learned of this he was furious, and protested to Governor Wentworth Rogers' absconding with the recruits, and also with the King's moneys from Massachusetts. The pleas fell on deaf ears and Rogers was left as a captain in the first company of the regiment. They left for Albany in late summer and were first employed in escorting provisions to "the Carrying Place," later to be called Fort Edward. (Loescher, 1946, p. 26.) Here he met Sir William Johnson, who at first embraced him as a much needed scout. Both were ambitious men, not above having the ends justify the means. Both were hungry for land, titles, and money. In later years, Sir William viewed Rogers as a threat to his ventures, and he became one of Rogers' many critics and foes.

After the defeat of the French forces at the September 8, 1755, Battle of Lake George, Rogers and his men helped in the construction and patrolling of the new Fort William Henry. Sir William, extremely anxious of the intents and size of the French force to the north, sent Rogers and others out on scouting missions. Of all Sir William's scouts, even the Mohawk Indians, only Rogers was successful and continued to bring back reliable information. Sir William learned that the French were not advancing, but were instead building a fort of their own at Ticonderoga ("Carillon"). As September passed into October and November, both sides were stalemated, busy fortifying themselves and not daring to advance. As the weather harshened in November, the bulk of both armies were withdrawn and the campaign season was over. (Loescher, 1946, p. 46.) Sir William left Fort William Henry under the command of a Colonel Jonathan Bagley with a winter garrison calling for 402 men. New Hampshire was required to staff 95 men, and these men elected Robert Rogers as their captain to carry the fight to the enemy. (Cuneo, p. 29.) It was in this role that Rogers found his niche in life. He did extraordinarily well in those first years, welding his small groups of men up to company size in raids against the French, penetrating the wilderness areas of Lake George, Lake Champlain, and points north—even into Canada.

In those days the military campaigns in North America ended with the onset of winter, and both sides settled down to cold, tedious, boring garrison life, both in the forts and in the cities where the troops were stationed. Rogers' scouts and raids changed all of that. Now the newspapers had news to thrill their readers: accounts of British success against the French in a normally dull time period. As the newspapers bestowed their laurels upon Rogers and his Rangers, the grateful citizens were in turn inspired to do as much. In Albany, a number of officers presented Rogers with a handsome set of clothes and 160 shillings to be laid out "in refreshments for him and his men." Later, in February, 1756, the New York General Assembly voted to award 125 milled Spanish pieces of eight to Captain Rogers for his "courage, conduct, and diligence." (Cuneo, p. 32.) In March, 1756, he was authorized by Governor Shirley of Massachusetts, then Commander in Chief of His Majesty's forces in North America, to recruit another sixty men for his Ranging companies, and was commissioned as captain of "His Majesty's Independent Company of American Rangers." (Cuneo, p. 33.) His new command was to be entirely different; it was not Provincial or Regular, but an independent corps attached to the British army, and on a pay scale sometimes exceeding that of regular troops. It was quite a feather in the hat of a person who, not too many months before, had almost been convicted as a criminal.

Rogers' early scouts and successes were the stuff that legends are made of. One of the earliest, known as the "Battle of Isle

Mutton" is well worth mentioning. Leaving Fort William Henry on the night of October 30, 1755, Rogers led thirty-three men armed with miniature cannon called "wall pieces" north in four bateaux down Lake George, and landed before dawn within a half mile of the enemy advanced camp. There they rested the entire day, and the next evening three Rangers brought back the information that the small camp was open to assault. Rogers dispatched these men, with seven Rangers who had become sick, up the lake to Sir William asking for a force to attack the camp. Two days later, while waiting for the hoped-for reinforcement, the Rangers were discovered by French scouts on land. Soon afterwards, two great canoes appeared, heading towards Rogers with over thirty Indians. Correctly surmising that he would be caught between land and water forces, Rogers was forced to choose between fleeing up the lake in his boats or making a stand and hoping that help would soon arrive. Surprisingly, he did neither. Embarking in his bateaux, Rogers led the Indians to believe he was preparing to flee; they in turn sped towards him with their canoes. It was just what Rogers had expected. The Rangers swung their boats towards the enemy and opened fire with the wall pieces, killing and wounding several Indians, partly sinking the canoes, and causing them to turn abruptly and flee for the safety of the French, who were coming to their aid. Rogers then turned his boats around and triumphantly rowed to Fort William Henry with only one man wounded. (Cuneo, p.24; Loescher, 1946, p. 42.)

On another scout at Carillon, Rogers managed to capture a French sentry by simply walking down the middle of the road pretending to be friendly. When the perplexed sentry called out "Que etes vous?" (Who are you?) he was answered "Rogers!" Rogers proceeded to disarm him and lead him away in capture. (Cuneo, pp. 43-44.)

In January, 1756, Rogers led seventeen men to Five Mile Point (a favorite ambush spot halfway between Fort Carillon and Fort St. Frederic), where they captured a sleigh, took two prisoners, and sent the horse, sleigh, and provisions through a hole in the ice to the bottom of the lake.

Another daring enterprise occurred in June, 1756. Rogers and his men rowed down Lake George under the cover of darkness in five newly arrived whaleboats; light, sturdy crafts which were fast like canoes. Landing somewhere near present-day Hulett's

Landing, they proceeded to spend the next four days lugging and carrying these boats over the mountains to the waters of Lake Champlain, four miles distant. Later they slipped past the French forts under the cover of darkness, and managed to capture and sink two French bateaux loaded with provisions for Fort Carillon. When the French later discovered the presence of the whaleboats on Lake Champlain, they were baffled. Believing that somehow the Rangers had discovered a secret water passage, they sent several parties of their own trying to find it. (Cuneo, p. 36; Loescher, 1946, p. 77.)

In January, 1757, Rogers, John Stark, and Captain Thomas Speakman led a force of more than seventy Rangers north towards the French at Fort St. Frederic. After a cold and tedious march of several days, the weather warmed and it began to rain. Fires were lit to dry out the wet muskets, and then early in the morning the Ranger force set out for the favorite ambush spot at Five Mile Point. Arriving there, they spied three provision sleds coming from Carillon en route to St. Frederic. Immediately dispatching Stark with one group to the far end of the land to stop the sleighs, Rogers had another group hold the center, from which the main attacking force would rush, while he himself would lead a third force out from behind to cut off any retreat. Not long after Stark and the others headed for their respective positions, Rogers observed a larger group of horsedrawn sleighs, far behind the first. Trying to warn Stark not to spring the ambush too soon, so as to alert the following contingent of sleighs, Rogers sent a runner in frantic haste towards Stark and his men. He was too late and the trap was sprung. Seeing their comrades captured, the following French sleighs abruptly wheeled about and fled back to Carillon to warn the garrison, where Commandant Lusignan dispatched about one hundred men northwest to find the Rangers' tracks and to lay down an ambush if they should be foolish enough to return the same way. They were.

Ignoring one of the most important rules of forest warfare, Rogers' Rangers returned to the sight of the previous night's campfires, rekindled the coals into fire, and again dried out their muskets. After a quick meal, they headed back south by way of their original route for the safety of Fort William Henry. Quite a few would not make it.

The French and Indian force had found the northward bound tracks of the Rangers about three miles northwest of the fort.

They followed them for a distance until they came upon a ravine that was an excellent spot for an ambush, and waited there silently, hoping for the Rangers to appear. They were not to be disappointed.

About an hour later, the Ranger force was seen heading back through the ravine. When the English were inside the killing ground, the trap was sprung.

Fortunately for the Rangers, over half of the French guns failed to fire because of the rain. Springing forth, the French troops charged among the Rangers, using bayonet and tomahawk. Rogers' men turned and fled back up the far slope to where John Stark and other Rangers had stopped and were now able to cover their comrades' retreat. The Rangers re-grouped on this hill and fought the French to a standstill until darkness came, when they made their escape. Rogers' casualties were: thirteen killed (including Speakman), seven captured, and nine wounded, including himself. It was Rogers' first rebuff in the woods war that made him famous. (Cuneo, pp. 45-50; Loescher, 1946, pp. 111-139.)

In the summer of 1757, Rogers and most of his Rangers embarked on the abortive campaign against Fortress Louisbourg. While the British were thus occupied on an ineffectual military operation, the French and Indians launched their successful assault against Fort William Henry, causing its surrender in August.

In the fall of 1757 Rogers and his Rangers began to have troubles with the British. In the early years of the corps, Rogers had men whom he could trust and rely upon to obey commands. As the war progressed and additional companies were added, problems with discipline began to surface. In November, 1757, British Captain Abercrombie and some regular officers accompanied some Rangers on a scout and immediately were made aware of the Rangers' attitude towards them. Unwilling to take orders or advice, the Rangers galled their counterparts by ignoring Rogers' own Ranging rules. They fired at game on the march, posted sentries at night who promptly went to sleep, argued constantly with the British, and feigned getting lost. All things considered, the scout was an embarrassing failure that the British made note of. It was not to be forgotten. (Cuneo, pp. 61-62.)

In December, two Rangers were accused of stealing rum from the British and were consequently tied to the whipping post and lashed. In response to this, indignant Rangers assembled one evening, chopped down the post, and threatened mutiny. The riot was finally put down, but Rogers was called down to answer for it. (Cuneo, pp. 62-64.) Now the British army started looking at the questionable discipline and usefulness of its Rangers. Colonel Thomas Gage then proposed the idea of raising a regiment of regulars, trained in forest tactics like the Rangers, but led by British officers and incorporated into the regular army. It was to be the start of the British light infantry. (Loescher, p. 214.)

It was not only the Rangers who did not follow their own rules for ranging; sometimes Rogers himself ignored them. Returning home by the same route (as in the first battle on snowshoes) proved a costly mistake for Rogers. Another costly mistake occurred in August, 1758, after the English were defeated at Carillon. French and Indian war parties took the offensive in a series of spectacular and devastating raids. After one particularly disastrous massacre near Half-way Brook, General Abercromby dispatched a force of 700 men to pursue the raiders and make a sweep of the country around South Baye. (Loescher, 1969, p. 16.) Failing to catch or encounter any enemy parties, Rogers and his combined force made camp near the ruins of old Fort Anne. The next morning, before getting underway in their return to Fort Edward, Rogers relaxed his caution and engaged in a contest of marksmanship with Ensign William Irwin of the regulars. (Loescher, 1969, p. 17.)

The shots reached the ears of the French partisan leader, Marin, who was not too far away with a smaller force of nearly 500. Marin set his men in an ambush at the head of a clearing that he knew the Rangers would take en route back to their fort. When the English column started to enter the forest, Marin sprung the trap. The leading men, including Israel Putnam, Lieutenant Tracy, and three Connecticut provincials, were overwhelmed and immediately made prisoners. The firing erupted, driving the English force back and strewing the ground with the dead from the powerful fusillade. The British regrouped and under Rogers' guidance began to bring their numbers up in advantageous positions, outflanking the ambushers. The battle raged for over an hour until the French wisely decided to disperse and retreat back towards Carillon. More than forty of Rogers' men were killed and at least that many were wounded. He killed as many of the enemy force, however, and retained the field. His carelessness in causing the ambush and subsequent death of many Connecticut men did not go unnoticed, and was reported by the surviving Connecticut men as soon as they returned to the fort. His judgment was subject to question. (Loescher, 1969, pp. 19-20.)

Not only was Rogers' judgment subject to question, but sometimes so were his reports, especially those concerning enemy numbers in battles. The infamous "body counts" of the Vietnam War, designed to impress military leaders and the press, had precedent. Rogers used inflated enemy figures throughout his career to keep his star shining brightly, both in victory or to salvage sympathy for a defeat, as in the Battle on Snowshoes.

In September, 1759, Rogers led a force of almost 200 Rangers north in a grueling march to attack and destroy the Abenaki village of St. Francis (now present-day Odanak, in the Province of Quebec). Attacking at dawn on October 6, Rogers and his men surprised the village, killed its inhabitants, and put it to the torch. Hastily retreating homeward, they were pursued by parties of French and Abenakis furious for revenge. Some Rangers were ambushed and killed, others were captured, but the bulk of the force got away only to fall prey to starvation, which claimed many. Some Rangers eventually turned to cannibalism, to keep from starving. (Cuneo, pp. 110-111.) Rogers, in his later reports of the raid, claimed to have killed from 200 to 300 Indians. (Loescher, 1969, pp. 56-65.) Modern-day evidence places the total kill at less than forty. (Day, p. 16.)

Robert Rogers' star of fame reached its zenith in the French and Indian War, and in the following war of Pontiac's Rebellion. From there it plummeted to disgrace. Rogers was placed in a debtors' prison in Southwark, England, and ended up dying there. The epitaph from the May 18, 1795, issue of the *London Press* noted his passing as follows: "Lt. Col. Rogers, who died Thursday last in the borough, served in America during the late war, in which he performed prodigious feats of valor. He was a man of uncommon strength, but a long confinement in the rules of the King's bench had reduced him to the most miserable state of wretchedness." (Cuneo, p. 278.)

THE LEADERS:
LANGY

I HAVE chosen to use the English spelling of Langy over the French spelling, Langis, because it is more widely recognized today and because it is closer phonetically to the real pronunciation ("Lahn-gee"). His complete name is Jean-Baptiste Levreault de Langis de Montegron. Sometimes he is recorded as Montegron or Levreault, but mostly he appears as Langis in the French reports and letters. (DCB, Vol. III, p. 399.)

Langy was born and baptized in the town of Batiscan, south of Quebec. His mother, Marguerite-Gabrielle de Vercheres, was descended from the lineage of the family that produced the famous Canadian heroine Madeleine de Vercheres. In the early years of New France, Madeleine's village (Fort de Verchere) was attacked by an overwhelming force of Iroquois warriors. Running as fast as she could to a small stockaded blockhouse, Madeleine shut the gates and took over the defense. She was only fourteen years old at the time. (Costain, pp. 447-449.) Her force consisted of two young boys and two feeble old men. They managed through bravery and strategy to hold off the Iroquois for a week until they were relieved. One might assert that this same bravery was passed on through generations and ended up in the blood of Langy. It would serve him well throughout his career.

His father was Leon-Joseph Levreault de Langis, a lieutenant in the Colony Marines. Langy and his three brothers, Alexis, Levreau, and Fontenelle, all attained the rank of lieutenant in their careers. (DCB, Vol. III, p. 399.)

I believe that Langy's ancestry and the military background of his family helped produce what I consider to be the best partisan leader in the forest battles and raids of the Seven Years' War. Considering the caliber of his comrades such as Marin, St. Luc de La Corne, Wolfe, etc., and his adversaries such as Rogers, Stark, and Putnam, this is perhaps a tough billing to fill. But I believe the records of Langy's accomplishments will bear that out.

Langy, in all probability, learned the craft of *le petit guerre* (the little war) during the years of King George's War, 1743-1748. He would have been a 20- to 25-year-old cadet. In 1748, he received his promotion to ensign second, and in 1751 was promoted to ensign first.

As the hostilities opened in 1755, Langy was stationed at Fort Beausejour near the present-day border of New Brunswick and Nova Scotia. (DCB, Vol. III, p. 399.) In June, 1755, a combined force of New Englanders and British regulars lay siege to the fort in an effort to drive the French from the Acadian peninsula.

The siege itself did not last very long, helped undoubtedly by the ineptness and cowardice of its commander, Louis Duchambon de Vergor. (Pothier, pp. 16-17.) After the fort was surrendered, Vergor was made to face a court-martial in Quebec.

Unfortunately for New France, Vergor, because of the influence of the corrupt Intendant Bigot, was acquitted. This same dull knave, Vergor, was later placed in command of an outpost on the Plains of Abraham outside the walls of Quebec City. His outpost was strategically placed on the cliffs to prevent British access to the Plains, should they be foolish enough to try and scale the heights. The British *were* foolish and daring enough to attempt this, and Vergor, who could have held them off easily until help arrived, was caught asleep in his tent. The rest is history. (Pothier, pp. 35-36.)

Returning to the siege of Fort Beausejour, it is interesting to find an account of bravery recorded in the diary of Jacau de Fiedmont, the French artillery officer stationed there. He noted that during the English bombardment, a small force of French and Acadians managed to block the entrance to the fort and then reinforced the adjacent curtains. This was accomplished by the Marine officer, Montegron de Langy, whom Fiedmont described as "an extraordinarily brave officer." (Pothier, p. 28.) It is the first recorded instance of Langy's daring. It would not be the last.

Langy was paroled with the others of Fort Beausejour and returned to Quebec by way of Louisbourg. Early in 1756 he married Madeleine de Manthet, widow of Jean-Jarret de Verchers. (DCB, Vol. III, p. 399.) Soon after, he went with his brother Alexis to gather information about enemy activity in the areas around Fort William Henry and Fort Edward. In June, 1756, Langy took a prisoner near Fort Oswego and remained there with Richerville, helping to draw up attack plans for the approaching army of Montcalm, which lay siege to the forts and caused them to surrender on August 14, 1756. (DCB, Vol. III, p. 399.) In October, 1756, near Fort Edward, Langy led a force of Indians which fell upon a party of Englishmen who were chopping trees. Langy's force killed about twenty and captured half a dozen. (DCB, Vol. III, p. 400.)

In a letter to the Chevalier de Levis dated August 17, 1756, Montcalm evaluated his partisan leaders. "Remember that Mercier is an ignorant and foolish man, St. Luc is a braggart and pratting, Montigny admirable but a pillager. Ligneris, Villiers, and Lery good. Marin brave but foolish, Langy, excellent. All the rest aren't worth mentioning." (Gallup and Shaffer, p. 40.)

In July, 1757, Levis sent Langy and his Indians to scout between Carillon and Fort William Henry, where they surprised two separate enemy scouting parties. (DCB, Vol. III, p. 400.) Langy accompanied Levis and Montcalm's army to the siege and subsequent surrender of Fort William Henry in August, 1757. The August 22 entry of Bougainville's journal recorded the French casualties suffered during the siege. Also included is a startling entry. "On the fourteenth day, they broke the head (executed) of a soldier of the Regiment of La Sarre who was found wanting in respect to the Sieur de Langis, Officer of Colony troops." (Bougainville, p. 178.) For a French regular soldier to be executed for insubordination to a Colony Marine officer was very rare indeed.

On November 2, 1757, Montcalm wrote to Governor Vaudreuil in praise of Langy, "Sieur Langis de Montegron has never ceased being used for the most interesting of scoutings, also the most laborious, and who has always distinguished himself." This is unique, because Montcalm and Vaudreuil disliked each other intensely, and constantly argued and bickered over almost anything. Yet they both found common ground in recognizing the exploits of Langy.

After the famous Battle on Snowshoes in March, 1758, Langy appeared to become the nemesis of Rogers' Rangers, constantly a thorn in their side. Burt Loescher, the great author of the books, *History of Rogers' Rangers* (1969) and *Rogers' Rangers: Genesis,* (1946), praises Langy as "the most famous of the French Canadian partisans," "the Rangers' most daring rival," and the "Rangers' most daring adversary." (Loescher, 1969, pp. 8, 83.)

In late June, 1758, the English and Colonial armies under Generals Abercromby and Howe were preparing to sail north to take Carillon in a massive assault. Rogers' Rangers were ordered out in advance parties to reconnaissance. One party of seventeen

Rangers and two lieutenants were ambushed in their whaleboats in the second narrows of Lake George by Langy and his Indians. They were taken by Langy to Bourlamaque, who commanded at Carillon, for questioning. (Bougainville, p. 220.) Learning of the impending English force being readied against them, Bourlamaque dispatched Langy and the prisoners to Governor Vaudreuil in Montreal.

As he made his way up Lake Champlain, Langy met the southward bound flotilla of French troops including Montcalm, Bougainville, and their staff. Reaching Montreal on June 29, Langy passed on the information to Vaudreuil, turned over his prisoners, and headed back to Carillon with the Indians, all eager to have a hand in the upcoming battle. They were not to be disappointed.

Upon reaching the fort, Langy was immediately employed by Montcalm in scouting duties. The July 4 entry in Bougainville's journal noted the following: "This evening there departed, under the orders of Sieur de Langis a detachment of 150 men, 104 of them volunteers from our regular battalions, 25 Canadians and a score of Indians. A fact worth noting and one which does us honor is that in this detachment, a Captain and seven Lieutenants of our regulars march under the orders of an Ensign; M. de Langis has only this rank. His orders are to go and observe the location, the number and the movements of the enemy at the end of Lac St. Sacrement and to make prisoners if possible." (Bougainville, p. 224.)

On July 5, 1758, the same journal records, "At five o'clock in the evening Sieur de Langis; detachment returned, having seen on the lake a great body of enemy barges which could only be what it was, the advance guard of their army, led by Colonel Bradstreet and Major Rogers." (Bougainville, p. 226.) Further in the same journal entry: "Consequently Sieur de Langy has been detached with 130 volunteers to take post between Mont Pelee and the lake, and Sieur de Trepezac, Captain in the Bearn regiment, supports him with three light companies." (Bougainville, p. 226.)

The 15,000 man army under Abercromby and Howe landed in the early hours of dawn on the northwest end of Lake George and proceeded to follow Rogers and his Rangers down the west side of La Chute River, intending to come in behind the French advance posts. Because they were too late to prevent the British landing, Langy's and Trepezac's forces attempted to make their way back to Carillon by a circuitous route through the mountains. Unfortunately they became entangled and lost in the trackless swamps below. However, they were not the only force that had managed to have gone astray. Rogers with his vanguard of 500 Rangers and Lord Howe's brigade were also lost. As the two groups blundered into each other, firing erupted and the French were caught between the falls of La Chute River and the two British forces. The fighting was savage; 150 French were killed and 150 were taken as prisoners, Langy received a leg wound while crossing the river under the covering fire of French grenadiers who arrived on the opposite bank. (O'Callaghan; Vol.X, pp. 751, 895.)

In this skirmish the British casualties were comparatively light; only about fifty were killed and wounded. Unfortunately for the British they lost their real commander, Lord George Augustus Viscount Howe. Now the critical decisions had to be made by the doddering old General Abercromby, whom events proved unfit for the task.

On July 8, 1758, the bloody battle of Ticonderoga erupted when the small French forces under Montcalm repulsed and soundly defeated the overwhelming force of British regulars, Highlanders, Provincials, and Rangers. It was in this battle, standing with Levis at the right of the French lines, that Langy was wounded twice more. (Bougainville, p. 238.) Langy and the Canadians made two sorties and took the charging English columns in the flank. Abercromby, appalled at the devastating loss of over two thousand of his best men, retreated down the lake, taking his army and Rogers' Rangers with him.

After the July battle, French and Indian raiders struck southward in ambushes against the English at Fort Edward, Saratoga, Half-way Brook Post, and the camp at the end of Lake George near the ruins of Fort William Henry. They were led by St. Luc de La Corne, Sabrevois, Marin, and of course, Langy. These raids continued throughout the summer and fall. On October 7, 1758, Bougainville noted: "On the seventh Sieur de Langy de Montegron left for the end of the bay for a raid with a detachment of forty men, twelve of them Indians." (Bougainville, p. 288.)

Bougainville left for Montreal on October 18. He stated "I took with me a prisoner captured by Sieur Langy Montegron between Fort Edward and Albany. His statement positively contradicted what they so firmly believed at Montreal." (Bougainville, p. 291.)

(The Canadian governor believed rumors that the English were going to mount another offensive at Carillon. Langy's prisoner gave proof that the English were already withdrawing the bulk of their troops towards Albany.)

In November, the French themselves withdrew the bulk of their troops, leaving Captain Hebecourt again in command at Carillon with 350 regulars, 100 marines, and 50 Canadians and Indians, probably led by Langy. (Bougainville, pp. 292-293.) On May 19, 1759, Langy was noted again as having taken several prisoners near Fort Edward. (Pouchot/Dunnigan, p. 178.) After this raid, Langy seems to disappear from the pages of history. There are reports of a Langy engaged in skirmishes with the Rangers who were burning habitants' homes, farms, and churches in the parishes above and below Quebec.

The year 1760 was indeed a bleak one for Canada. Forts Duquesne, Frontenac, Niagara, Carillon, St. Frederic, and even mighty Quebec had fallen to the English. Montcalm was dead and New France was on her knees gasping and expiring. Most French and Canadians were in despair and ready to give up. But not those men like Langy.

Robert Rogers was returning from Albany to the new British fort at Crown Point in February 1760. As he neared the five-mile point between Ticonderoga and Crown Point, he smiled and told his recruits of some of his successful ambushes there. Unfortunately for Rogers and the recruits, he took too much for granted, as far as safety. First, this war was not yet over. Second, for some inexplicable reason, the recruits were not armed; their 32 new muskets were still in cases in Rogers' sleigh. Third, and most unfortunate for the Rangers, was Langy and his Indians, lying in ambush there.

When he recognized Rogers in the first sleigh, Langy delivered a murderous volley that killed most of the horses, rendering the sleigh useless. Rogers, sensing judgment day, fled madly towards Crown Point. Many of the new Rangers were not as fortunate; five were killed and four were taken prisoner. After watching the familiar back of Robert Rogers disappear towards Crown Point, Langy felt recompensed when he discovered the booty on Rogers' sleigh. There were 32 new muskets, 100 hatchets, 55 pairs of moccasins, and 11,961 pounds of New York currency -- the payroll for troops at Crown Point. Of this, 3,961 pounds was Rogers' own money. (Loescher, 1969, p. 84.)

Six weeks later, Langy made his successful raid near Crown Point. Here he captured Lieutenant Fortescue and Ensign Stuart of the British regulars, Captain James Tute of the Rangers, and six enlisted men, all without firing a shot. (Loescher, 1969, p. 85.) He took them to Montreal, and returned to Isle Aux Noix.

The last mention of Langy is in Pouchot's journal, and it is a sad one for Canada. Pouchot states, "It was from that position (Isle Aux Noix) in the winter, they formed raiding parties which always brought back a number of prisoners. Langis made some further raids in the spring. This officer, the best leader of raids among the colonial troops, was unfortunately drowned while trying to cross a river in a canoe with two of his men." (Pouchot/Dunnigan, p. 258.)

And so, into history went the incredible Langy. His name should be placed among the very bravest and most capable of the French Canadians who fought like lions against the overpowering might of the British empire.

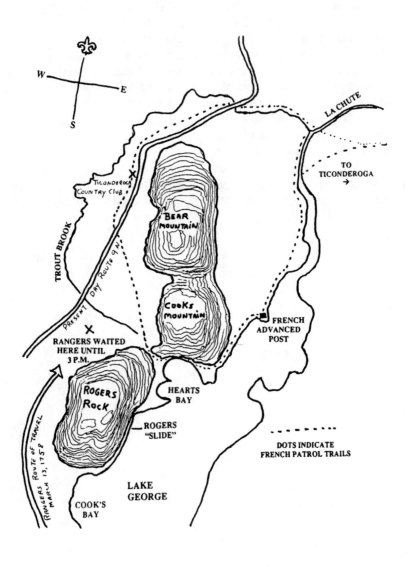

W—E

S

LA CHUTE

TO TICONDEROGA →

TROUT BROOK

PRESENT DAY ROUTE 9 NT

TICONDEROGA COUNTRY CLUB

BEAR MOUNTAIN

COOKS MOUNTAIN

FRENCH ADVANCED POST

X
RANGERS WAITED HERE UNTIL 3 P.M.

ROGERS ROCK

HEARTS BAY

ROGERS "SLIDE"

- - - - - - - -
DOTS INDICATE FRENCH PATROL TRAILS

RANGERS ROUTE OF TRAVEL MARCH 13, 1758

LAKE GEORGE

COOK'S BAY

II. OVERALL VIEW OF THE BATTLE AREA

7. LOCATION

TERMING the "Battle on Snowshoes" and the "Battle of Rogers Rock" together is a misnomer. Rogers Rock as we know it today was called Mont Pelee by the French and Bald Mountain by the English. Both sides used it as a landmark because of its easily seen bare rock face. No battle was ever fought there.

Present-day "Rogers Rock" is approximately four miles south of the actual site of the battle. The adjoining series of hills to the north that appear on today's topographical maps, Cook's and Bear mountains, had no names in those days. The actual battle site was on the lower northwestern slopes of today's Bear Mountain, slightly north of the Ticonderoga Country Club.

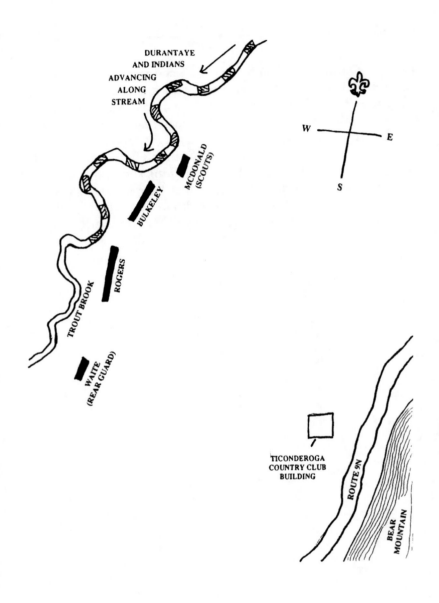

DURANTAYE
AND INDIANS
ADVANCING
ALONG
STREAM

W — E

S

MCDONALD
(SCOUTS)

BULKELEY

ROGERS

TROUT BROOK

WAITE
(REAR GUARD)

TICONDEROGA
COUNTRY CLUB
BUILDING

ROUTE 9N

BEAR
MOUNTAIN

1. ROGERS' RANGERS' AMBUSH

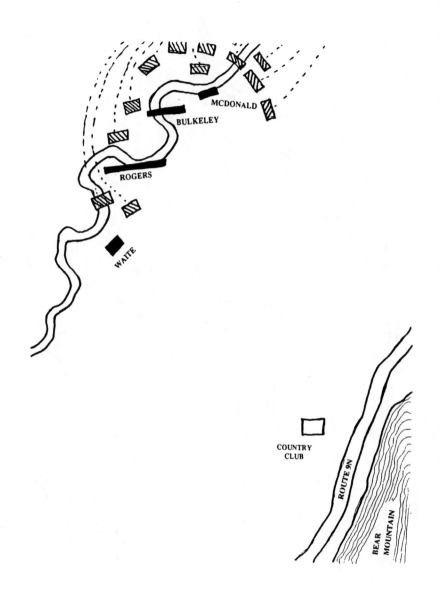

MCDONALD

BULKELEY

ROGERS

WAITE

COUNTRY CLUB

ROUTE 9N

BEAR MOUNTAIN

2. LANGY'S COUNTERATTACK

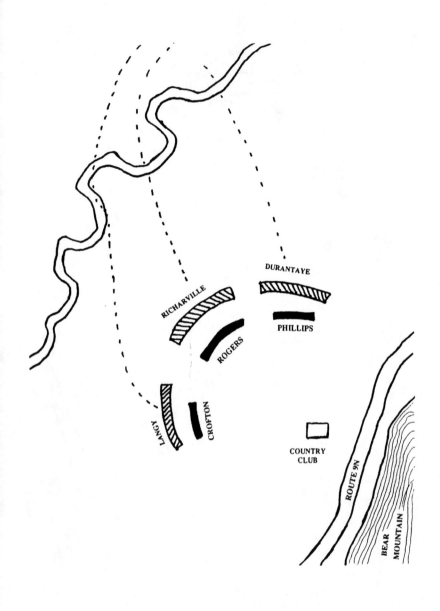

DURANTAYE

RICHARVILLE

PHILLIPS

ROGERS

LANGY

CROFTON

COUNTRY
CLUB

ROUTE 9N

BEAR
MOUNTAIN

3. RANGERS DRIVEN UP THE HILL

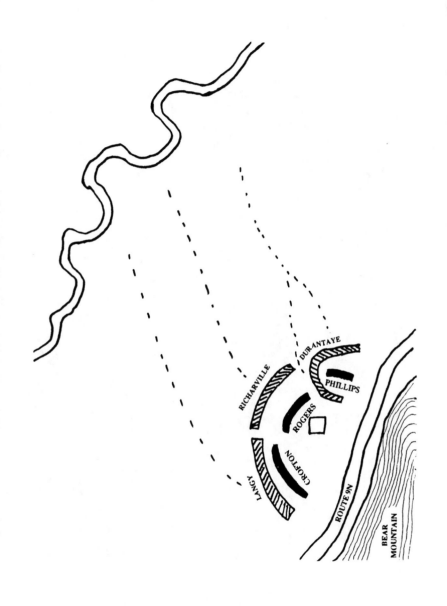

4. DURANTAYE CUTS OFF PHILLIPS FROM THE MAIN FORCE

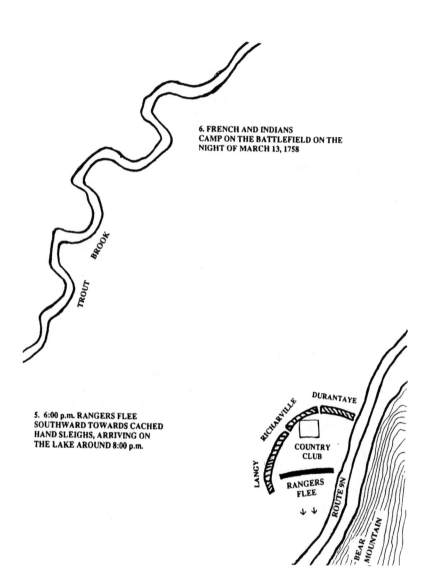

6. FRENCH AND INDIANS CAMP ON THE BATTLEFIELD ON THE NIGHT OF MARCH 13, 1758

TROUT BROOK

5. 6:00 p.m. RANGERS FLEE SOUTHWARD TOWARDS CACHED HAND SLEIGHS, ARRIVING ON THE LAKE AROUND 8:00 p.m.

DURANTAYE

RICHARVILLE

LANGY

COUNTRY CLUB

RANGERS FLEE

ROUTE 9N

BEAR MOUNTAIN

5. RANGERS FLEE SOUTHWARD;
6. FRENCH CAMP ON THE BATTLEFIELD

8. The Battle

March 13, 1758
6:00 A.M.

THE black inkiness of the night was relenting, dawn was only an hour away, and Captain Robert Rogers was glad of it. The night had been cold and damp, and with no fires to keep warm, it had been a long one.

He had been extremely nervous on this scout because of the events of the past few weeks. One was the infuriating fact that Colonel Haviland had announced to the public that Rogers was to be sent out to the French forts with a great force of men. Close on the heels of that was the capture by the French of a sutler's servant who was in a convoy of wagons out of Fort Edward, bound for Albany. Another man had mysteriously disappeared or deserted on a scout that had just returned from Ticonderoga, or Carillon, as the French called their fort. But what had unnerved Rogers the most was his recent encounter with the French partisan leader, Wolfe, at Fort Edward last month. Wolfe had come down under a flag of truce to try and negotiate the release and return of prisoners on both sides. While he was there, Rogers took the opportunity to rib the French officer about his recent raid on Carillon, and the receipt he had left for the commandant on the horn of one of the oxen he had slaughtered. This feat had elevated Rogers' already inflated ego among the British and Provincial troops alike, and he enjoyed the opportunity to tease the French leader about it. But the only recognition Wolfe gave to Rogers was a fixed grin and a slight nod of his head. As the partisan officer was about to leave, he turned to Rogers, and fixing his frosty blue eyes on him, said in a low measured voice full of warning, "Take care the next time you come to visit." The cold blast of air was not the only thing that caused Robert Rogers to shiver that day. Because of all this, Rogers was taking no chances.

This morning, it was agreed that instead of continuing on the ice, the Rangers would don their snowshoes and proceed overland, keeping the mountains between themselves and the French outposts at the head of the lake. They were on their way by 7:00 A.M. and continued along to the west side of Bald Mountain, which the French called Mont Pelee. Here they left Rangers Cunningham and Scott to watch the cached hand sleighs, and to warn them of any enemy who might follow on their backtrack. The Rangers then proceeded onward through the forest valley, which the French called the "Route des Agniers" or Mohawk Trail, keeping the steep slopes of Bald Mountain on their right.

Meanwhile, down the lake, a party of six Abenakis was returning from a scout near Fort Edward. They were tired and cold and eager to reach Fort Carillon, where they could rest and feast with their red brothers and the French soldiers. Almost certainly they would receive some brandy for their efforts, which of course they would exaggerate. As they moved along over the black, windswept ice of Lac St. Sacrement, they noticed something beneath their feet: innumerable crystalline slivers of ice, created by a legion of men wearing ice creepers as they traveled over the frozen lake. Following their direction, the Abenaki leader turned his head to the left, where the morning rays of the sun helped show where the wall of snow on the western shore had been broken down to clear a pathway for the men. Silently the six Indians made their way towards the shore. As they neared the edge of the lake, they became as deer approaching a pond for a drink; nerves taut, eyes searching, ears straining for the slightest movement that would betray a hidden enemy. Not far into the woods, under a stand of hemlocks, they found where the Rangers had camped the night before. Snowshoe tracks led away towards the valley behind the mountains on the west side of the lake. They had seen enough. Returning to the ice they started in haste to the fort, in that easy, tireless lope that the Indians and Canadians had used for generations.

11:00 A.M. Robert Rogers signaled a halt to his men, and posting sentries they settled down for a rest and cold meal. At about the same time in Fort Carillon, not more than five miles away, Langy and Durantaye were returning to the room they were sharing. They had breakfasted with Captain d'Hebecourt, Cadet Richerville, and other officers of La Reine and the Marine. The warm bread from the ovens was excellent, and the porridge, sweetened with the maple *sucre* and washed down with wine, had gone a long way in restoring their strength from their recent exertions. Sieur La Durantaye had just arrived on the twelfth from

Montreal with a group of 200 domesticated Indians, and they were eager to strike south in raids against the English near Fort Edward and Saratoga. However, the Indians first demanded huge quantities of food and brandy, a fact that did not please Captain d'Hebecourt. Langy was there resting between successful raids at Fort Edward and he enjoyed talking with Durantaye, who, he knew, looked up to him with friendly rivalry. The conversation was the same as always for young men at war away from home. They talked of their adversaries, the English—especially the Rangers. They talked of the weather, the forests, they talked of Canada; but mostly they talked of their wives, sweethearts, and families back home. As they talked with full stomachs, enjoying the warmth of the fire, the noise of the soldiers outside going about their daily tasks grew softer. They drifted back to sleep. It was 11:30 A.M.

Rogers' men were encamped in a huge stand of pines on the northwest slope of Bald Mountain, where they could look ahead and see the notch and the next rise of mountains to the north. Somewhere in that notch ran a trail that the French were known to send a daily patrol through, that circled and made its way back to the fort. Rogers and his officers decided to wait until about 3 o'clock in the afternoon, when they judged the patrol should be back at the fort, and they would then move to the other end of the valley where they would pick an ambush spot for tomorrow morning's patrol. With sentries posted on all sides, a few of the Rangers rummaged in their packs for jerky, parched corn, cheese, or bread, and then washed it down with swallows of grog from their canteens. Most, however, rolled up in their blankets, sought out a patch of sun, and dozed off into a fitful sleep. Unknown to many, it would be their last.

1:00 P.M. The six Abenakis were fast approaching the fort and its sprawling village of huts and tents below. Sharp-eyed Crees, Nipissings, and Caughnawagas sensed the urgency of the approaching Abenakis, and set up a whoop that quickly turned into a clamor of shouts as the entire village ran up to see what it was about. Perhaps they thought that a vision foretold by the Indian sorcerer was about to come true. As the leader plunged doggedly on to report to the French commander, the others stopped, and between labored breaths told of their discovery of the approaching force of Rangers. Instantly hell appeared to have come to earth as the entire assemblage of Indians broke into an ungodly clamor of screams and whoops, and the scene at the fort became one of bedlam.

The terrific din awoke Langy and Durantaye with a start. Dressing quickly, they rushed outside, only to encounter d'Hebecourt and Richerville coming towards them at a run. Below, the courtyard quickly filled with screaming Indians, white coated marines and regulars, and Canadians with their red tuques and blue capotes. Trying to raise his voice above the noise below, d'Hebecourt relayed to his partisan leaders the message the Abenakis had just brought in. Rangers, 200 of them, were only four miles away.

As Captain d'Hebecourt stood on the west demi-lune of Carillon watching the last of Langy's force disappear over the hill, he glanced at the lemon colored sun starting its descent, and figured the time to be about 1:30 P.M. In his mind he replayed the events of the past hour. He remembered the screaming mass of Indians who rushed madly towards the village below, eager to be on their way, stopping only to grab muskets, tomahawks, and knives. These were the worst of the lot, already besotted with drink, whipped into a frenzy by the sorcerer, and, undoubtedly, they would have left without any French leadership had not Durantaye and a few Canadians eagerly jumped at the chance to strike the first blow. He also remembered how Langy grabbed his young friend's shoulder, telling him to wait until the entire force was ready, but seeing that this was impossible, bade him to be careful and promised to follow immediately with a larger force. While Durantaye and the Indians boiled out of the fort, Langy and d'Hebecourt managed to bring a semblance of order to the chaos, directing the Indian chiefs to get extra powder, balls, and supplies, while they assembled the regulars of La Reine and the Compagnie Franche Marine troops. Langy's Canadians were ready to go.

D'Hebecourt asked for volunteers from the soldiers to accompany Langy, and was overwhelmed by the enthusiastic response. Not wanting to weaken the fort's defenses however, in case the Rangers were a diversion for a more serious attack, d'Hebecourt limited the aroused troops to a few dozen. The rest he placed on alert. Shortly all was ready and Langy followed Durantaye's group of 96, with his own force of 205. They were not more than one-half hour behind Durantaye.

3:00 P.M. If a raven had flown high, far into the sky above the peaks of Mont Pelee, Cook's, and Bear mountains that day, he would have been witness to a scene about to unfold that was unlike any other he would ever see. Far below on the west slope of Mont Pelee, hundreds of green-coated and blanketed men were rising from their resting place. Some were rolling their blankets and putting on their packs. A small group of men, three to be exact, was already crossing the notch and heading onto the slopes of Cook's Mountain, with Trout Brook below them on their left. Soon the entire force of green-coated men would follow in two divisions.

At the northern end of Bear Mountain the raven could have looked down and seen a line of men appearing on snowshoes, strung out for over one hundred yards. They were wearing brown deerskins and blankets of red, blue, and green. A few men with white blanket coats and blue capotes were among them. Farther to the east, another larger group was fast catching up to the first. They were already making better time on the firm snow that the lead group had packed, and now they were only one-half mile behind. Far in the distance the raven would see the walls of Fort Carillon. From within, thin white plumes of smoke rose straight up from the chimneys. There was no wind on this day.

As Ensign McDonald and his two scouts plodded along in the deep snow, their eyes were fixed mainly ahead and below towards the small ice-covered brook. The soft shuffling of the snowshoes and the labored breathing of the men were the only sounds in the forest today. Strange, thought McDonald, it's like a tomb. No wind whistling, no squirrels chattering, no bluejays squawking. Even that raven high above was not making a sound. Coming along a slight ridge, the Rangers spied a huge snow-covered boulder and made for the shelter of it to take a rest and catch their breaths. They had not been there long when they suddenly spied movement far down the slope in a clearing. It was an Indian— make that two. Suddenly the clearing was filled with Indians and a few Frenchmen among them. They seemed uncertain as to what direction they would pursue. After a few moments' discussion, they started forward again, following the ice-covered brook back towards the notch. McDonald and his men realized that this would bring the Indians into contact with Rogers and the main force less than a mile behind. Staying hidden, they watched as the clearing emptied and, confident that no others were coming,

5. The Ranger Ambush on Trout Brook

turned back on their own snowshoe tracks at a run to warn Rogers and the rest of the Rangers. They were glad of the boulder and ridge that shielded their movements from the enemy below. They would not have been so glad if they could have known that the same boulder was now blocking another view: that of Langy and his force now entering the clearing. It was 3:30 P.M.

The Rangers were marching along in two divisions with Captain Bulkeley leading the first, followed by Rogers in command of the second. Ensigns Waite and White brought up the rear. They had covered a mile and a half by Rogers' estimate, when they suddenly saw McDonald and his scouts coming towards them at a run. Breathlessly they told of the force of Indians approaching them on the brook, and for the first time that day Robert Rogers grinned broadly. This was too good to pass up.

Rogers quickly told his officers and men to face left, lay down their packs, and hurry down the hill to the brook, where they were to hold their fire until he shot the signal gun. The Rangers quickly ran to cover behind trees and rocks, in hollows and ravines, and soon had a line of ambush that stretched well over one hundred yards. There, silent like the forest, they waited; nervous, hearts beating fast, eyes straining for the approach of their hated foes. This would be a turkey shoot. It was 3:45 P.M.

The Indians came along on the brook just as McDonald had said they would. They moved in that curious shuffling gait, eyes darting to the left and right. Rogers watched them come into his trap as a cat watches a mouse. A minute or two more, he thought, and it will be complete; his 180 Rangers should mow them down like a field of ripe corn. Suddenly the lead Indian stopped, and with him so did time. *Why* he stopped, is still a mystery. Perhaps he needed to rest, or to re-tie his *raquettes*, or to shift his blanket. Perhaps his eyes caught a movement or spied something out of place. No one ever knew. But one of the younger Rangers, whose nerve had finally broken down, shattered the stillness with a blast from his Brown Bess musket. The Battle on Snowshoes had finally begun. It was 4:00 P.M.

That lone blast had frozen everyone for a split second, then galvanized them into action. French and Indians did different things. Some, wary and warned by the lone shot, threw themselves behind trees, on the ground, or in the snow behind the banks, to escape the shuddering staccato blast that forty Brown Bess muskets roared out an instant later. Others, slower,

6. Langy's Counterattack

confused, or perhaps still befuddled from their drinking, were bowled to the ground like tenpins. Some were killed instantly, others were knocked off their feet, screaming and writhing in agony. Blood was everywhere; sprays of red and pink covered the snow behind and underneath the terrified men. Many, in shock, crawled and twisted desperately; trying to get away, leaving trails of blood, splinters of bone, and uncoiling loops of intestines. Some of the survivors returned the fire, others ran to the opposite bank for the cover of the trees, but most ran back up the brook the way they had come. Seeing his trap sprung too early, Rogers jumped up and in a loud roar yelled to Bulkeley and his men to "head 'em," before they could get away. The Rangers needed no prodding. The forty or so who had fired did not bother to reload. They charged into the creek bed, savagely wielding tomahawks and knives. Many stopped to take scalps, which were worth five pounds sterling back at Fort Edward. Other Rangers pushed and ran through the carnage, shooting and shouting, eager to overtake the enemy who was fast going out of sight around a turn in the brook. In their frantic pursuit they did not notice that the enemy ahead had stopped somewhat and was starting to return fire. The Rangers doubled their efforts to close the distance, and, as they rounded the slight curve of Trout Brook, they suddenly came face to face with the "Avenging Angel" of Carillon and his 200 men. At that instant many of the Rangers realized that they had made a terrible mistake, and for most, it would be their last.

Having heard the single shot, followed by the fusillade moments earlier, Langy deployed his men into a crescent front, and coming around that slight curve, slammed into the group of Rangers. The French and Canadians did not have to be told what to do; instinctively they leveled their fusils and fired into the tightly packed group of men on the creek bed before them. It was devastating. Over fifty Rangers were blasted instantly to the ground, and a dozen more, wounded slightly, began their panicky run back to Rogers and safety. As he saw the terrifying change of fortune, Rogers screamed for his men to fall back up the slope.

With a rush of yells and fire the French and Indians plunged on right behind them. Langy's Canadians had raced down the creek bed so swiftly that they had succeeded in cutting off the rear guard of Rogers' force. Only three men, including Ensign Waite, managed to flee to safety above. The Rangers, now having gained the advantageous higher ground, laid down a fusillade that temporarily stopped the French.

By this time, the fighting had settled down, in contrast to the madness of the previous moments. Both groups, like winded boxers, paused to catch their breath, and the firing died down to a few scattered shots.

Langy and Richerville quickly ran back through the carnage on the brook to find Durantaye shaken, but unscathed. All around them were members of the French force dispatching any wounded Rangers. Indian tomahawks slammed into skulls, crushing them like eggs, while French bayonets were driven deep into the ribs of their hated enemy. Blood lust overpowered any clear thinking on that fateful afternoon. The Indians, unpredictable in any situation, were fast going out of control now, due to the scalps of their brothers that, moments before, the Rangers had taken. Adding fuel to this flame were the canteens of rum that they had found and were quaffing greedily.

Deciding to use the drinking and charged emotions of the Indians to his best advantage, Langy instructed Durantaye to take the French left and Richerville the center, while he, Langy, would try to sweep around the right. With the French using the maddened Indians as hunting hounds to flush out the hidden foe, the Canadians were teaming up in groups of twos and threes to pick off any Rangers who showed themselves. The third phase of the battle was about to begin.

On the French left, Durantaye sent a group off to try and get around the Rangers' right flank, while Langy's Indians attempted the same on the other. All the while, Richerville directed concentrated fire from the middle of the line. Seeing this maneuver, Rogers sent Ensign Bill Phillips to secure the ground on the Rangers' right, and Lieutenant Crofton to do the same on their left.

The battle was now a continuous barrage of fire from both sides, and the heavy gray smoke hung in the windless air, stinging the men's eyes and obscuring their vision. Certain parts of the Ranger line were holding the French at bay with pockets of spirited resistance. One such group caught Langy's attention as he looked upward to a small knoll where four or five Rangers were yelling taunts and derisions between shots, led by a huge bearded Ranger in a green jacket with silver buttons.

A movement to his left caught Langy's eye and he spotted his three favorite Canadian marksmen: Gabriel, Jacques, and Joseph. They, too, had noticed the giant and were waiting with primed fusils for his next appearance, steadying their aim by resting their guns on the tree behind which they hid. Soon the huge fellow finished reloading and with a curse upon the French dogs, jumped up looking for another target to shoot. He never got the chance. At that instant, three fingers tightened on three triggers and the resulting shower of sparks, followed by a bright flash sent three acorn-sized lead balls smashing into their foe.

One ball took him through the chest, spraying pink froth over his comrades and the snow behind them. The other two hit him squarely in the head, nearly decapitating him. As the three Canadians quickly dropped back behind the huge pine tree to reload, Jacques' eyes met Langy's and he grinned broadly. This Ranger's scalp would not be worth taking.

As the battle reached its climax, one clear fact began to assert itself. For each Ranger who tried to return fire at the outflanking French and Indians, two or three fusils would zero in on him. Eventually, in ones and twos the Rangers were being picked off by the superior marksmanship of the Canadians. Like a snowball rolling down a mountain, slowly at first and then gathering speed and momentum, the odds of the French force began to work against the Rangers.

While Crofton had temporarily managed to stop the assault on the Rangers' left flank, Phillips' party, in achieving the same with the Indians on the right, found themselves pulled out of position, an opening that Durantaye's force quickly exploited. In less time than it takes to tell, French Marines and Indians rushed upward to drive a wedge between Rogers and Phillips, and instantly Phillips' group found itself cut off and surrounded. Seeing the hopelessness of their position, Phillips' men threw down their muskets and asked for terms. Calling to his men to cease fire, while the captured Rangers were quickly bound to the trees with deerskin thongs, Durantaye yelled up to Rogers to surrender or perish in the assault. Viewing the situation, Rogers and his men answered the French and Indians with a heavy barrage of fire that drove Durantaye and his men back into cover, but not before a few Indians had buried their hatchets and knives into some of the bound Rangers. Phillips, still alive, awaited his fate as the battle raged around him. It was 5:45 P.M.

7. The Canadian Marksmen

8. Durantaye Calls for Rogers to Surrender

Both Rogers and Langy noticed the sun setting on the horizon, and both knew that darkness was coming fast. Rogers wanted to hasten its coming while Langy desperately wished to hold it back. Darkness was the only thing that would bring an abrupt end to this deafening, roaring madness.

By then, Rogers had perhaps sixty men remaining. As the French charged up the hill in the final assault, Rogers knew he would be overwhelmed if he tried to make a stand or retire in a large body. Cupping his hands he yelled for his men to run for it and head back to the lake, and they needed no further prodding. Instantly they jumped up, and, feeling the hounds of hell coming after them, dispersed in twos and threes for the safety of the lake, not four miles distant.

Some made it, some did not. In the graying darkness, even the superb shooting of the Canadians had fallen off. But enough lead balls flew up the slope to drop five or six more Rangers, and those who were wounded limped madly in a desperate struggle to get away. The Indians, running easily on their wide raquettes, caught up with those poor souls and made mincemeat out of them.

As the blue and purple sky faded into darkness, the stars started to appear with the pale moon of March. Save for a single musket shot and some hoarse shouts, the stillness was a welcome relief to the din of the battle. Looking down towards the brook, Langy could already see a few fires being kindled. His men, tired and exultant, started back down, talking excitedly among one another and helping wounded comrades along. In a few minutes Langy would meet with Richerville and Durantaye, and after assessing the situation would send them back to Carillon where d'Hebecourt would be anxiously awaiting news of the battle. They would take with them the wounded who could be transported back to the warmth and safety of the hospital and fort. Tonight Langy would camp on the field of battle, as was his right to do. Tomorrow he and his men would recover all the booty, and hunt down any survivors. As he started back down the forested slopes, Langy took in great breaths of the clear mountain air and mused to himself that he did not win the battle with darkness, but he had won this battle on snowshoes. The fires burning below matched the brightness of his smile.

March 14, 1758, 6:00 A.M. Langy awoke with a shiver. The night had been cold and damp. All around him men were waking up, rousing themselves with difficulty. Some were coughing,

9. The Morning Campfire - Langy, Gabriel, and Richerville

10. Langy Examines Rogers' Commission

others were standing up and relieving themselves, while over to his right a couple of Caughnawagas were vomiting from the copious amounts of rum they had swilled in last night's wild celebration around the fire.

Speaking of fire, there was Gabriel uncovering the ashes and exposing the glowing coals. With a handful of yellow birchbark, he coaxed them into flames and then added a handful of dry hemlock and pine twigs to the fire. The fire grew rapidly and already men were filling their brass kettles with water from the rivulet to boil for breakfast. Soon everyone was sitting, drinking hot tea and chocolate, eating bowls of hot mush and meal; and even then, one could smell the pipes of tobacco that were being smoked by the early risers. There was no hurry, men talked quietly and reposed in the slight warmth of the morning sun. They waited for the stiffness and soreness of their muscles to abate before they took to the hunt. Any Rangers who were able to get away would be long gone. Those who couldn't, would be found and dispatched.

As he sat there, Langy's thoughts took him back to a hunt in Canada with his father and his brother, Alexis, years before. They had wounded a bear towards nightfall, and the boys were eager to follow and finish it off, but their father wisely held them back. That night, sitting by the fire, he explained to them that if the wound was mortal, the bear was already dead not far into the swamp. If the wound was slight, he was already miles away. But if he was hurt badly enough that he could not run away, but was still alive, he would be in the swamp hiding and waiting for the hunters. Better to have the light of day to help them see him first, Papa explained sagely. The boys drifted off to sleep fitfully, eager for the coming dawn. The next morning after they awoke and ate, it seemed as Papa would never get going. Finally, all was ready and they took up the trail. What little blood sign there was showed up scantily, but enough to guide them. Suddenly Papa's sharp voice brought them up with a start, and he motioned to their right where a huge, decaying log lay. At first they saw nothing, but as they crept closer they saw the black bear lying stone dead next to the log. Unable to run any farther, he had circled back from the trail to await his tormentors. Fortunately, he had died in the night before the young Langy and his family caught up with him. It was a lesson that Langy had remembered always and had passed on to his men. Never chase after an enemy in the darkness. Too many things could happen, and most of them were bad.

As the men made ready to move out, the pipes were knocked against callused palms, muskets were re-loaded and re-primed, and fresh flints were locked into hammers. The French force was ordered to spread out, and the final hunt was begun. Only once was the stillness broken by the report of a French musket, as a Ranger was put out of his misery. The Indians would not waste their powder; a knife or tomahawk would do just as well.

Well before noon the entire force was back at the bivouac area, and men and sleighs dispatched from the fort were coming in from the east. This was good, Langy thought, as he turned and looked at the wounded men and the piles of muskets, knapsacks, hats, coats, canteens, and other items stacked on the ground before him. There would be plenty of booty for all. The Indians already had more than 140 red, dripping scalps hanging at their belts. Langy himself was holding a green coat, trimmed with silver lace, obviously that of an officer, that one of his Indians had found on the slopes. Langy felt inside the pocket and pulled out a piece of paper that, surprisingly, turned out to be the commission of Langy's opponent, Captain Robert Rogers, signed by General Shirley. Langy felt that somewhere on that blood-strewn battlefield lay the body of his adversary, the best of the English partisan fighters. A few months later, Langy and the French realized that Robert Rogers had survived, and would do battle with them again.

Finally all the goods were piled and lashed on the sleds. Many men carried a captured musket as their portion of the spoils of war, to keep or to trade with the Indians. As the column plodded down the packed trail to Fort Carillon, Langy's mind drifted back, and he replayed the exciting events of the past two days. He was finally awakened from his reverie when the cannon of the fort boomed out its salute to the victorious French force returning to the safety of its walls. Men were lining the ramparts and demi-lunes, cheering lustily for the tired champions of the forest war. As he emerged from the tunnel, the sparkling green eyes of Langy met those of Captain d'Hebecourt, who returned a flashing smile to the Canadian partisan leader. In that instant of time both knew that the I.O.U. left by Captain Robert Rogers in December had finally been paid in full.

9. AFTERMATH

ROGERS and his men passed the next two days in sharp contrast to the victorious French. After darkness ended the battle, the Rangers made their way back to the cached hand sleighs where Rogers met them on the lake at about eight o'clock. Immediately he dispatched two men (probably the two Rangers who had stood guard over the sleighs) in haste to Fort Edward for help. He then selected eight more men who were in relatively good condition to pull four hand sleighs, each containing a severely wounded Ranger. He sent these men southward on the lake to the rendezvous point. (Cuneo, p. 78.)

Rangers continued to come in during the night and in the early hours of dawn. Finally, at daybreak, Rogers and his remaining force fled down the lake, lest they be discovered and pursued by the French.

His messengers arrived at Fort Edward at noon on the fourteenth. Immediately, Captain John Stark and a relief party left with three horsedrawn sleighs filled with provisions and blankets, and met Rogers' force at Hoop Island, six miles north of where Fort William Henry had stood less than a year ago. (Cuneo, p. 79.) After spending the night there, the Rangers resumed their trek and arrived at Fort Edward on the fifteenth. A provincial soldier noted in his diary, "About 5 o'clock I see Ye Maj'r com in Him self being in ye rear of ye whol. This was a vast cold and tedious day especially for ye wounded men." (Fitch, p. 53.) The silence of those troops who watched the spectacle was the extreme opposite of the heady reception of Langy's men at Fort Carillon.

Four of the severely wounded Rangers died of their wounds shortly afterwards at Fort Edward. The British volunteers, Capt./Lt. Pringle and Lieutenant Roche, surrendered to the French at Fort Carillon on March 20, after wandering lost in the mountains for six days after the battle. (Another source gives the wandering men's names as Creed and Kent.) Rogers' servant, who tried to be their guide, started hallucinating and apparently lost his mind. One night he wandered away from Pringle and Roche and died of exposure. These two men, along with the captured

Phillips are the only prisoners known to have survived. (Parkman, pp. 362-363.)

In his reports, Rogers estimated the enemy force to be 700 men. Crofton put the estimate at 700 to 1000. This was simply not so, and even the most dyed-in-the-wool Rangers researchers and buffs usually admit it. Only one modern writer supports Rogers' claim.

I have several thoughts on the disputed number of men involved in the battle. First, it was common for both sides to exaggerate enemy numbers, especially after losing a battle. This numerical increasement of the odds makes you look better and your defeat a whole lot easier to take.

Secondly, Rogers may have *believed* that there really were that many French and Indians coming at him. After all, who has the time to count in a battle with bullets coming at you from three directions. Some evening, try counting people while sitting at a high school or college basketball game. After you finish, remember this: you are sitting in a fixed spot, counting others in fixed spots, in a safe and well-lit environment; much different from the conditions Rogers and Crofton faced.

A third reason to believe that Rogers overestimated the number of French and Indian troops is that the garrison of Fort Carillon in winter consisted of 330 to 350 men. After Fort William Henry was burned to the ground, Carillon became the farthest twig on the branch of the Champlain Valley supply line. The farthest. It was hard enough just to provision the garrison. The idea of further stretching the resources of Carillon in the dead of winter, by taking on 500 to 700 Indians expecting to be fed and outfitted, was out of the question. Food was scarce in Canada after two successive years of poor harvest. Add to that the strangulation of supplies from France by the British navy, along with the thievery and rapine caused by the corruption of Intendant Francois Bigot and his knaves, and the specter of starvation became a real threat for the French soldier and civilian alike. It was so bad that the people of Quebec were limited to four ounces of flour a day, while in Montreal the women refused to eat the horsemeat that was issued to them. They rioted, and induced some of the soldiers of La Marine to riot also. It took diplomacy and force by the Chevalier de Levis to put an end to the protests. (Bougainville, p. 195.)

Finally, d'Hebecourt would not have sent out a huge force of soldiers that would have put the fort in jeopardy by inviting a possible surprise attack. Indeed, the fort commandant of the year before, Lusignan, had been reprimanded for doing just such a thing. Bougainville, in his journal, noted, "The success of this affair cannot excuse M. de Lusignan from having weakened his garrison considerably, and thus running the risk of being taken by a surprise attack." (Bougainville, p. 82.) His reference is to a smaller forest battle in January 1757, between Rogers and the French, not too far from the scene of the 1758 Battle on Snowshoes. As far as we can ascertain from the information available, the figures stand thus: Durantaye had 96 men, and Langy had 205 men that fateful day.

Let us finish this story by answering the question, Did Rogers escape, as legend tells it, by sliding down the sheer precipice known today as "Rogers' Slide"? I doubt it emphatically. I have no hesitation in stating here that I would bet everything I own, or ever have owned, against his doing it. Here are the reasons why:

1. Rogers never, *ever*, said or claimed that he did it, nor were there any reports or mention of such a feat by Rogers, or any of his men. With his ego and reputation for bravado, I'm sure he would not have let such a feat go unmentioned.

2. The battle was ended by simultaneous darkness and the scattering of the Rangers. Now why, in all good sense, would the Indians give chase? Everyone involved had just fought a physically, mentally, and emotionally charged battle. From the Ticonderoga Country Club (the accepted site of the battle) to the state campground at Rogers Rock (near where the sleighs were cached) is four miles by road. Taking different zig-zag routes, or going over the notch between Cook's Mountain and Rogers Rock into Hearts Bay and around on the ice to the rendezvous site, is probably that far and more. Why, if you were an Indian that day, would you chase these fleeing survivors in the dark? Over 130 bodies were lying back there in the snow, whose scalps and gear were yours for the taking at no danger to yourself. How far would you have chased the survivors? One mile, two perhaps? If you were chasing these men in a foot race, would it take you that long to catch them? How about if they went of sight? (Pretty easy to do in the woods in the dark.) Would you continue on, and run into an ambush of muskets spitting buckshot? Why even take the chance of a branch poking out your eye, or an ankle twisting on

the slippery, uneven ground? Like the wounded bear in the previous chapter, these Rangers could turn at bay and snuff out your life like a candle. I doubt seriously if the Indians ever gave chase for more than a few hundred yards.

3. If Rogers was the great woodsman he is acknowledged to be and "knew the country like the back of his hand," he would never have brought himself up on a mountain called "Bald" because of its sheer rock face. That's the equivalent of knowingly running into a box canyon.

4. I have spent a great deal of my life on snowshoes, and I know what can be done and what cannot. It is very hard, if not impossible, to climb up very steep slopes, and Rogers and his Rangers did not have the exceptional snowshoes and bindings we possess today. They would have taken the easiest route available, which was the direction they originally came from, and which was already packed down. Or they would have run over the notch to Hearts Bay and the lake.

5. Another much-repeated tale, like the Rogers' Slide myth, claims that Rogers threw down his jacket with his commission in it "to slow down the Indians." Come on, who are we kidding here? Most of the French-led Indians couldn't speak English, and I doubt if any of them could read it. It is a fact that Rogers lost his uniform coat that contained his commission from General Shirley. I do not subscribe to the idea that he tossed it aside to slow the pursuing savages. Most likely he took it off at the start of the battle, near the ambush site, and did not have time to recover it in the heat of battle. Or perhaps it fell from his pack as he ran. I do not believe he would have intentionally thrown away an outer coat that could have been the prevention of his freezing that night.

6. My theory, based on years and years of travel over the battle site, patrol trail, Rangers' route, etc., is this: I believe Rogers and a few others probably fled alongside Cook's Mountain, swung to the left through the notch, and came out on the lake near Hearts Bay. This is exactly the opinion to which my friend and long-time historian of the Ticonderoga area, Roger De Chame, subscribed. Climbing a hill, even a small one, is harder than descending, but not as dangerous. My guess is that Rogers took a spill or a fall coming down (as I and many others have done), and when he reached the Rangers at the rendezvous site at eight o'clock one of them may have asked, "How did you get here, Cap'n? Rogers

might have said in reply, "Over the back of Bald Mountain. I slid halfway down on my arse getting here," or words to that effect. As the Rangers talked among themselves that night, and in later conversations, his statement may have taken on a new and different meaning.

Robert Rogers had been known since his youth as being tough and strong, brave and far sighted, and brash and arrogant. He had plenty of reasons to be. He and John Stark were the best Rangers the British ever had. He was a tremendous leader of men. But he was not an idiot. To suggest he slid down a sheer precipice of rock and ice, on snowshoes, after dark, to a frozen lake over 500 feet below, is to say that he was a fool. Robert Rogers deserves better than that.

EPILOGUE

HISTORY can be very unkind to its makers. Here we have Langy, revered by the Canadians, loved by the Indians, honored by Montcalm and the French regulars, and feared and respected by the Rangers. He was wounded at least three times that we know of, victorious in three out of four engagements facing Robert Rogers and his Rangers, proudly promoted in rank by the Canadian Governor Vaudreuil, and favorite scout of the Marquis de Montcalm. He lost his life in April 1760, while preparing for the final vain defense of his country. Beloved son, husband, and brother, he remains buried in the parish of St. Antoine de Padua of Longueil, Quebec, without even a gravestone or marker. Canada should be ashamed.

On the other hand we have Robert Rogers. Entering the army under suspicion of counterfeiting, he eventually rose to the rank of major in the British service and commanded a corps of Rangers. He became hated and distrusted by his former commanders and friends, and after the war, was charged and imprisoned for suspected treachery. As his monumental drinking and debts continued to increase, the American Revolution approached. Then, it seems, he offered his services to both sides, apparently holding out for the highest bidder. The British, with whom he finally threw in his lot, despised and looked down on him for his drunkenness and dissolute living, and ultimately relieved him of his command. He not only abandoned his wife and child, leaving his family to face all creditors, but turned against his own friends and neighbors when he fought for England. He ended up in a debtors' prison and died a raving alcoholic. Yet movies have been made of him, books written about him, and in New York State a campground, an island, and a mountain have been named for him.

Compared to Langy, it just doesn't seem right.

GLOSSARY

CURTAINS - In fortification, is that part of the body of the place, which joins the flank of the bastion to that of the next.

DEMI-LUNE - In fortification, is a work placed before the curtain to cover it, and prevent the flanks from being discovered sideways; it is made of two faces, meeting in an outward angle.

GLACIS - is the part beyond the covert-way, to which it serves as a parapet and terminates the field in an early slope at about 20 fathom distance.

GILL - is a four-ounce ration of rum, issued on a daily basis, usually to work details and scouts.

MILICE - French word equivalent to militia.

RE-DOUBT - Is a square work without any bastions, placed at some distance from a fortification, to guard a pass, or to prevent an enemy from approaching that way.

RAQUETTES - French word equivalent to snowshoes.

SCOTCH-BONNET - A full knitted woolen cap descended from the Kilmarnock style. These were highly sought after by the Rangers.

SUTLER - In war, one who followed the army and furnished provisions for the troops. When camped they pitched tents or built huts.

SAPPERS - Soldiers belonging to the Royal Artillery, whose business was to work the sap, which was a trench, to approach the fort within firing range.

BIBLIOGRAPHY

BEAROR, BOB. "Langy, The Best There Ever Was." *Muzzle Blasts,* Vol. 56, No. 2. October 1994.

BIRD, HARRISON. *Battle for a Continent.* New York: Oxford Press, 1965.

BOUGAINVILLE, LOUIS ANTOINE de. *Adventure in the Wilderness.* Edward P. Hamilton, editor and translator. Norman: University of Oklahoma Press, 1964.

BOUCHARD, RUSSEL. "Les Fusils de Tulle en Nouvelle France 1691-1741." Chicoutimi, Quebec: *Journal des Armes enr.,* 1980.

BOURLAMAQUE, FRANCOIS CHARLES de. *Letters de M. de Bourlamaque au Chevalier de Levis.* Quebec, Canada: Demers & Frere, 1891.

BROWN, M. L. *Firearms in Colonial America.* Washington: Smithsonian Institution Press, 1980.

CHARTRAND, RENE. "The French Soldier in Colonial America." *Historical Arms Series.* No. 18. Ottawa: Museum Restoration Service, 1984.

COSTAIN, THOMAS B. *The White and the Gold.* New York: Doubleday & Co. 1954.

CUNEO, JOHN R. *Robert Rogers of the Rangers.* Fort Ticonderoga, New York: Fort Ticonderoga Museum, 1988.

DAY, GORDON M. "Rogers' Raid in Indian Tradition." *Historical New Hampshire.* 1982.

DeLISLE, STEVEN. Letter to Bob Bearor concerning the death certificate of M. de Langis. Jan. 16, 1991.

____. Letter to Bob Bearor concerning the promotions of M. de Langis, June 1991.

____. Letter to Bob Bearor concerning the family of M. de Langis, June 14, 1991.

____. Letter to Bob Bearor concerning the personal effects of M. de Langis, June 22, 1994.

DICTIONARY OF CANADIAN BIOGRAPHY (DCB) Vol. III. Toronto: University of Toronto Press. 1974.

ECCLES, WILLIAM J. *The Canadian Frontier, 1534-1760.* University of New Mexico Press, 1974.

FITCH, JABEZ JR. "The Diary of Jabez Fitch Jr. in the French and Indian War." 1757. Publication No. 1. Rogers Island Historical Assn.

GALLUP, ANDREW, and DONALD SCHAFFER. *La Marine: The French Colonial Soldier in Canada, 1745-1761.* Bowie, Maryland: Heritage Books, Inc., 1992.

HAMILTON, EDWARD D. *The French and Indian Wars.* New York: Doubleday & Co., 1962.

HICKS, MAJOR JAMES E. *French Military Weapons. 1717-1938.* N. Flayerman & Co. 1964.

JAMIESON, PAUL. *The Adirondack Reader.* Glens Falls, New York: Adirondack Mountain Club, 1982.

KALM, PETER. *Travels in North America, 1748-1751.* English Version. New York: Dover Publications, 1987.

LANCASTER, BRUCE. *Ticonderoga, Story of a Fort.* Northstar Books, 1962.

LEWIS, MERIWETHER L. *Montcalm, The Marvelous Marquis.* Vantage Press, 1961.

LOESCHER, BURT G. *History of Rogers' Rangers.* San Mateo, California: Privately printed, 1969.

LOESCHER, BURT G. *Rogers' Rangers: Genesis.* San Mateo, California: Privately printed, 1946.

NICOLAI, MARTIN L. "A Different Kind of Courage; The French Military and the Canadian Irregular Soldier During the Seven Years' War." *Canadian Historical Review*, Vol. LXX, No. 1. Toronto: University of Toronto Press, 1989.

O'CALLAGHAN, E. B., editor. *Documents relating to the Colonial History of the State of New York*. Vols. IX and X. Albany: Wered & Parsons, 1858.

PARKMAN, FRANCIS. *Montcalm and Wolfe*. New York: Collier Books, 1962.

POUCHOT, PIERRE. *Memoirs on the Late War in North America between France and England*. Translated by Michael Cardy. Edited by Brian Leigh Dunnigan. Old Fort Niagara Association Inc., 1994.

POTHIER, BERNARD. "Battle for the Chignecto Forts, 1755." *Canadian Battle Series*, No. 12. Toronto, Canada: Balmuir Books, 1995.

RUTLEDGE, JOSEPH L. *Century of Conflict*. New York: Doubleday, 1956.

SMITH, CLYDE H. *The Adirondacks*. New York: Viking Press, 1976.

SMITH, Capt. George. *Universal Military Dictionary*. 1755. Ottawa: Museum Restoration Service. 1969.

SMITH, JAMES. *Scoouwa: James Smith's Indian Captivity Narrative*. Columbus: Ohio Historical Society. 1978.

STOTT, EARL. *Exploring Rogers' Island*. Fort Edward, New York: Rogers' Island Historical Society, 1986.

WHITE, WILLIAM CHAPMAN. *Adirondack Country*. New York: Alfred A. Knopf, 1983.

INDEX

Appendix:

Account of the Battle on Snowshoes from Rogers' Journals, which appeared in the London Chronicle of January 7-9, 1766. Also, French versions of the battle: Montcalm's account to the War Minister, M. de Paulmy, on April 10, 1758, and Adjutant Malartic's account.

The London Chronicle for 1766
Vol. XIX No. 1413

Jan 7-9

JOURNALS of Major ROBERT ROGERS: Containing an account of several excursions he made under the Generals who commanded upon the Continent of North America during the late war.

I N some of our former papers we have given an account of and extracts from, this brave Officer's *Concise History of North America;* and at present and hereafter occasionally, we shall insert some passages from his *Journals*, which contain many material particulars never before published. In the introduction to this work, the Major with extreme modesty cautions the reader to consider, "That it is the soldier not the scholar, that writes; and that many things here were wrote, not in silence and leisure but in desarts, on rocks and mountains, amidst the hurries, disorders and noise of war, and under that depression of spirits which is the natural consequence of exhausting fatigue."

These journals commence as early as September 24, 1755, and end February 14, 1761, and contain a very circumstantial account of the numberless fatiguing and dangerous excursions the Major was employed in during that time; in all which he acquitted himself with the utmost intrepidity, fidelity and judgment.

In the year 1758, the Major was ordered by Lord Loudon to march with 400 men against the French forts. However, the number was afterwards lessened; and on the 10th of March in that year by orders from Col. Haveland, he began his march from Fort Edward for the neighbourhood of Carillon with 180 men only, officers included. The 11th and 12th nothing material occurred. What happened afterwards in this excursion is thus related by our author:

The 13th, in the morning, I deliberated with the officers how to proceed, who were unanimously of opinions that it was best to go by land in snow-shoes, lest the enemy should discover us on the lake; we accordingly continued our march on the west side, keeping on the back of the mountains that overlooked the French advanced guards. At twelve of the clock we halted two miles west of those guards, and there refreshed ourselves till three, that the day-scout from the fort might be returned home before we advanced; intending at night to ambuscade some of their roads, in order to trepan them in the morning. We then marched in two divisions, the one headed by Captain Bulkley, the other by myself: Ensigns White and Wait had the rear-guard, the other officers were posted properly in each division, having a rivulet at a small distance on our left, and a steep mountain on our right. We kept close to the mountain, that the advanced guard might better observe the rivulet, on the ice of which I imagined they would travel if out, as the snow was four feet deep, and very bad traveling on snow-shoes. In this manner we marched a mile and an half, when our advanced guard informed me of the enemy being in their view; and soon after, that they had ascertained their number to be ninety-six, chiefly Indians.

We immediately laid down our packs, and prepared for battle, supposing these to be the whole number or main body of the enemy, who were marching on our left up the rivulet, upon the ice. I ordered Ensign M'Donald to the command of the advanced guard, which, as we faced to the left, made a flanking party to our right. We marched to within a few yards of the bank, which was higher than the ground we occupied, and observing the ground gradually to descend from the bank of the rivulet to the foot of the mountain, we extended our party along the bank, far enough to command the whole of the enemy's at once, we waited till their front was nearly opposite to our left wing, when I fired a gun, as a signal for a general discharge upon them; whereupon we gave them the first fire, which killed above forty Indians; the rest retreated, and were pursued by about one half of our people. I now imagined the enemy totally defeated, and ordered Ensign M'Donald to head the flying remains of them, that none might escape; but we soon found our mistake, and that the party we had attacked were only their advanced guard, their main body coming up consisting of 600 more, Canadians and Indians; I then ordered our people to retreat to their own ground, which we gained at the expence of fifty men killed; the remainder I rallied, and drew up in pretty good order, where they fought with such intrepidity and bravery as obliged the enemy (tho' seven to one in number) to retreat a second time; but we not being in a condition to pursue them, they rallied again, and recover'd their ground, and warmly pushed us in front and both wings, while the mountain defended our rear; but they were so warmly received, that their flanking parties soon retreated to their main body with considerable loss. This threw the whole again into disorder, and they retreated a third time; but our number being now too far reduced to take advantage of their disorder, they rallied again, and made a fresh attack upon us. About this time we discovered 200 Indians going up the mountain on our right, as we supposed, to get possession of the rising ground, and attack our rear; to prevent which I sent Lieutenant Philips, with eighteen men, to gain the first possession, and beat them back, which he did: and being suspicious that the enemy would go round on our left and take possession of the other part of the hill, I sent Lieutenant Crafton, with fifteen men, to prevent them there; and soon after desired two gentlemen, who were volunteers in the party*, with a few men, to go and support him, which they did with great bravery.

The enemy pushed us so close in front, that the parties were not more than twenty yards asunder in general, and sometimes intermixed with each other. The fire continued almost constant for an hour and half from the beginning of the attack, in which time we lost eight officers, and more than 100 private men killed on the spot. We were at last obliged to break, and I with about twenty men ran up the hill to Philips and Crafton, where we stopped and fired on the Indians, who were eagerly pushing us, with numbers that we could not withstand. Lieutenant Philips being surrounded by 300 Indians, was at this time capitulating for himself and party, on the other part of the hill. He spoke to me, and said if the enemy would give them good quarters, he thought it best to surrender, otherwise he would fight while he had one man left to fire a gun‡.

I now thought it most prudent to retreat, and bring off with me as many of my party as I possibly could, which I immediately did; the Indians closely pursuing us at the same time, took several prisoners. We came to Lake George in the evening, where we found several wounded men, whom we took with us to the place where we had left our sleds, from whence I sent an express to Fort

Edward, desiring Mr. Haviland to send a party to meet us, and assist in bringing in the wounded; with the remainder I tarried there the whole night, without fire or blankets, and in the morning we proceeded up the lake, and met with Captain Stark at Hoop Island, six miles north from Fort William Henry, and encamped there that night; the next day being the 15th, in the evening, we arrived at Fort Edward.

The number of the enemy was about 700, 600 of which were Indians. By the best accounts we could get, we killed 150 of them, and wounded as many more. I will not pretend to determine what we should have done had we been 400 or more strong; but this I am obliged to say of those brave men who attended me (most of whom are now no more) both officers and soldiers in their respective stations behaved with uncommon resolution and courage; nor do I know an instance during the whole action in which I can justly impeach the prudence or good conduct of any one of them.

* I had before this desired these gentlemen to retire, offering them a serjeant to conduct them; that as they were not used to show-shoes, and quite unacquainted with the woods, they would have no chance of escaping the enemy, in case we should be broke and put to flight, which I very much suspected. They at first seemed to accept the offer, and began to retire; but seeing us so closely beset, they undauntedly returned to our assistance. What befel them after our flight, may be seen by a letter from one of the gentlemen to the commanding officer, which I have inserted next to this account of our scout.

‡ This unfortunate officer, and his whole party, after they surrender'd, upon the strongest assurances of good treatment from the enemy, were inhumanly tied up to trees, and hewn to pieces in a most barbarous and shocking manner.

MONTCALM'S ACCOUNT *to the Minister, M. de Paulmy from Montreal, Apr 10, 1758*: 'Captain D'Hebecourt, of the regiment of La Reine, who commands at Carilon, having been informed, on the 13th of March, that the enemy had a detatchment in the field which was estimated by the trail to number about 200 men sent a like detachment of our domicilated Indians, Iroquois and Nepissings, belonging to the Sault St Louis and the Lake of the Two Mountains, who had arrived on the preceding evening, with some 30 Canadians and several cadets of the Colonial troops, under the command of Sieur de la Durantaye, of the same troops; Sieur de Langy, one of the officers of the colony, who understands petty war the best of any man, joined the party with some of the Lieutenants of our battalion, who are detached at Carillon. The English detachment consisted of 200 picked men, under the command of Major Rogers, their most famous partisan, and 12 officers. He has been utterly defeated; our Indians would not give any quarter; they have brought back 146 scalps; they retained only three prisoners to furnish live letters to their father. About four or five days after, two officers and five English surrendered themselves prisoners, because they were wandering in the woods, dying of hunger. I am fully persuaded that the small number who escaped the fury of the Indians, will perish of want, and have not returned to Fort Lydius. We have had two Colonial Cadets and one Canadian slightly wounded, but the Indians who are not accustomed to lose, have had eight killed and seventeen wounded, two of whom are in danger of dying.' - (Docs. R. C. H. N. Y, *X*, pp. 693, 697).

ADJUTANT MALARTIC'S ACCOUNT: 'A Cadet detached from Carillon, came to inform the General that M. La Durantaye's party had arrived the 12th, on which day an old sorcerer had assured them that they would see the English before long; on the morning of the 13th 5 or 6 Indian scouts came to say that they had discovered fresh tracks of 200 men, whereupon the chiefs raised the musterwhoop and set out immediately with their warriors, some soldiers and Canadians, who traveled nearly 3 leagues without meeting any one; suspecting that the English had taken the Falls road they took the same course; M. Durantaye, who had joined them at the Bald Mountain, was with the van guard; he received the enemy's first fire, which *made him fall back a little, and gave them time to scalp two Indians whom they had killed: meanwhile, M. De Langy, having turned them with a strong party of Indians, and having fallen on them when they felt sure of victory, had entirely defeated them; the Indians having discovered a chief's scalp in the breast of an officer's jacket, refused all quarter, and took 114 scalps; the opinion is, that only 12 or 15 men escaped, and that this detachment was composed of 170 or 180, commanded by Captain Rogers, who is supposed to be among the killed.'* - (Docs. Rel. Col. Hist. N. Y., X, pp. 837-838).

Author Bob Bearor, center, portrays Langis in a re-enactment of the Battle on Snowshoes, with sons Cliff, left, as Richerville, and Ted, right, as Durantaye.

ABOUT THE AUTHOR

Bob Bearor started shooting muzzleloaders in 1968, and started hunting with them in 1976. In 1979 he began period camping and trekking. He took a 13-point buck with his .45 caliber flintlock for a record in 1980. An experienced Adirondack hunting guide, his articles have appeared in many national and local hunting and muzzleloading magazines.